mountaineers
outdoor
basics

Wilderness GPS

A Step-by-Step Guide

GPS

Bob Burns
Mike Burns

MOUNTAINEERS
BOOKS

This book is dedicated to the memories of the teachers of navigation who have gone before us, including Clinton M. Kelley, Richard B. Kaylor, Erhard Wichert, and Scott Fischer. Without their knowledge and leadership, some of us would still be lost in the wilderness.

Mountaineers Books is the publishing division of The Mountaineers, an organization founded in 1906 and dedicated to the exploration, preservation, and enjoyment of outdoor and wilderness areas.

MOUNTAINEERS BOOKS

1001 SW Klickitat Way, Suite 201, Seattle, WA 98134
800.553.4453, www.mountaineersbooks.org

Printed in the United States of America
Distributed in the United Kingdom by Cordee, www.cordee.co.uk
First edition, 2013

Copy editor: Joeth Zucco
Book design: Mountaineers Books
Cover design, layout, and illustrations: Jennifer Shontz, www.redshoedesign.com

Cover photograph: *Hiker on a summit* (Photo by Liz Chen, iStockphoto)

Library of Congress Cataloging-in-Publication Data
Burns, Bob, 1942–
    Wilderness GPS : step-by-step guide / Bob and Mike Burns.
        pages cm
    Includes bibliographical references.
    ISBN 978-1-59485-762-1 (pbk)—ISBN 978-1-59485-763-8 (ebook)
1. Orienteering—Equipment and supplies. 2. Navigation—Equipment and supplies.
3. Outdoor recreation—Equipment and supplies. I. Burns, Mike, 1970– II. Title.
    GV200.4.B86 2013
    796.58—dc23
                                                            2013018768

ISBN (paperback): 978-1-59485-762-1
ISBN (ebook): 978-1-59485-763-8

Contents

Acknowledgments

The authors wish to express their appreciation to a number of individuals who contributed significantly to this book. First of all, Ron Gailis, whose cooperation with us on numerous field trips, as well as his extensive research into the Global Positioning System and "smart" devices, has greatly enriched this text. We also wish to acknowledge Mountaineers Books staff, particularly Margaret Sullivan and Laura Shauger, and Mountaineers climber and GPS user John Bell (coauthor with Bob of the navigation chapter of *Mountaineering: The Freedom of the Hills*, 8th edition), Chuck Haberbush, Jim Giblin, Stan Jacobs, Dave Matthes, and Donnie Hatch of DeLorme, Inc.

Preface

The origins of this book lie in the first mention of the use of the Global Positioning System (GPS) in the navigation chapter of *Mountaineering: The Freedom of the Hills*, 6th edition, 1997 (*Freedom 6*). Together we crafted that chapter of *Freedom 6* as a mix of traditional techniques and a new look at navigation and routefinding. We also wrote the navigation chapter for *Freedom 7* in 2003, with a more detailed and updated explanation of the use of the GPS in wilderness navigation.

In 1997 we approached Mountaineers Books with the idea that this chapter could be extracted as a text for navigation classes and seminars that The Mountaineers was conducting. Our suggestion led to the creation and publication of the first edition of *Wilderness Navigation* in 1999. This new book contained much more detail regarding the use of the GPS than that contained in *Freedom 6* and *Freedom 7*.

The accuracy of the GPS changed significantly on May 1, 2000, when the US government turned off selective availability, thereby increasing the accuracy of the GPS from a point within a sphere the size of a football field to a point within a racquetball court. This led to changes so significant that a second edition of *Wilderness Navigation* was published in 2004.

Mountaineers Books approached us in late 2011 to craft a new text, devoted entirely to the GPS. *Wilderness GPS* builds on the knowledge base of *Wilderness Navigation* but with a more detailed treatment of the GPS.

This knowledge base can be made even better by your experience. Please feel free to check in with us and to share your GPS navigation experiences, insights, and any suggestions for improvement on our Twitter page: Wilderness_GPS, or join the GPS discussion on Facebook at Wilderness Gps. We look forward to hearing from you.

In the following text, the device that you hold in your hand will interchangeably be referred to as a GPS "unit," "receiver," or "device," but never as "a GPS." Remember, GPS is an acronym for the Global Positioning System (emphasis on the word *system*), which includes the satellites, numerous ground stations and computer servers, and many users. A GPS unit (or receiver or device) is a relatively simple radio *receiver* tuned to receive signals from the GPS satellites.

Introduction

Where am I? How can I find my way from here to there? How far is it to my destination? Will I be able to find my way back? These are the questions we posed in *Wilderness Navigation*. The Global Positioning System (GPS) can be used to answer all of them, precisely.

Due to increased interest in GPS technology with more advanced receivers, computer connectivity, downloadable maps, news media, law enforcement, missing persons, search-and-rescue, and the ever-evolving subject of GPS usage with "smart" or mobile devices (separate from a dedicated GPS unit), the need for an accessible, straightforward text as a supplement to the GPS receiver's quick start guide and owner's manual is apparent.

The GPS is an amazing technology. It can provide your exact point position on the surface of the Earth: the ultimate objective of orientation (as opposed to a more inferior line position or an even weaker area position). But the GPS is not perfect. In fact, the weakest link in the system may be the users themselves! Practice with your GPS receiver is important. The GPS receiver will not do the navigation work for you. If you carry a GPS receiver for emergencies only, and find yourself hopelessly lost without knowing how the receiver works, or without having taken the simple step of saving a good waypoint at the trailhead, and you are out of cell phone range, good luck!

After you purchase a new GPS receiver, read the quick start guide furnished with most receivers, and eventually read the entire owner's manual front to back, as boring as it may be. All receivers are different in their user interfaces, and we cannot possibly explain how to use all of the different functions across all the different brands and models. What we will do is thoroughly explain the GPS and how to maximize the usefulness of your GPS device.

We have our own quick start guide to using your GPS receiver in the wilderness:

1. Install fresh batteries and carry spares.

2. Download maps of the intended travel area, if your receiver allows, and carry a paper topographic map and compass.
3. Obtain and save a solid 3-D position fix at the trailhead or other starting point.
4. Ensure that the position displayed on your device makes sense to you.
5. Ensure that someone back home knows your travel itinerary.

With these five simple steps (which will be detailed in the chapters to follow), you will be less likely to become a statistic or, even worse, end up the subject of a tragic story on your local evening news.

In this book, we explain how to obtain a good, trustworthy GPS position fix, describe the Universal Transverse Mercator (UTM) and latitude/longitude coordinate systems, and show you how to plot a position on a map using both. You will learn how to determine the distance and direction from your position to your intended destination and how to travel in that direction, how to save any position as a waypoint for future use, and how to cope with some of the potential problems, pitfalls, and limitations of GPS technology. Finally, we will explain a number of techniques to minimize battery power consumption when using either a dedicated GPS receiver or the GPS function of a smart device.

We would like to begin by recalling three true stories that illustrate how the GPS can be used in wilderness travel, along with examples of some difficulties and limitations.

THE CHIWAWA RIVER

On the last day of a scenic loop trip through Glacier Peak Wilderness, we had intended to ford the Chiwawa River at the only feasible crossing area for miles in each direction. For a variety of reasons, we became lost and unable to find the crossing. Due to heavy forest cover, we could not see any landmarks to help us determine our location, and we could not see or hear the river. We took the GPS receiver out and let it acquire a position. After several minutes it locked onto three satellites and gave us a position in UTM[1] coordinates (see point A on fig. 1):

10 6 63 335E
53 21 305N Elevation 6480 feet

---

[1] The UTM coordinate system is easier to use and is more accurate than the better-known latitude/longitude system. See appendix A for a complete explanation of UTM.

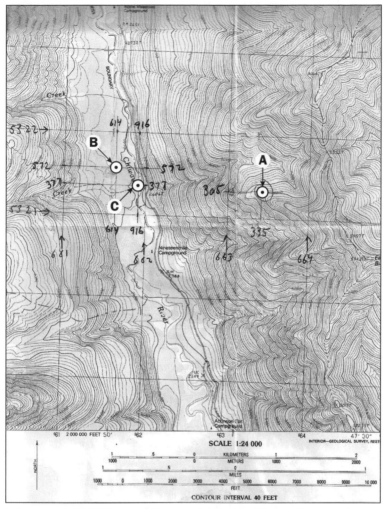

Figure 1. Part of USGS topographic map showing the Chiwawa River crossing area

We could tell that this position was not where we were. First, the elevation was 4000 feet too high, since those with altimeter watches all agreed with the map elevation of about 2500 feet. Second, when we double-checked the indicated GPS position and plotted it on the map, it was far across the wide and deep river, which we knew we had not yet crossed. From this we concluded that we had an unreliable 2-D position fix, and we had to find a more open place with a better view of the sky.

We walked east for a short time, found a small clearing, and again turned on the GPS receiver. After a few minutes it gave us the following position (see point B on fig. 1):

10 6 61 614E
53 21 572N Elevation 2655 feet

This time we were far more confident of the indicated position, since the indicated elevation agreed with our maps, altimeters, and common sense. When we plotted the UTM coordinates on the map, they showed that we were less than a half mile northwest of the river crossing (point C). We therefore set a bearing of SE (135°) on our compasses and headed out in that direction, compasses in hand, through light forest and brush. After a short time we arrived at the river and could see the small parking lot across it!

Analysis: Without the GPS receiver we would have eventually found the river crossing, but the GPS receiver saved us hours or perhaps days of looking for it. The experience reminded us that GPS technology is far from perfect, and that it is essential to double-check any displayed GPS position and altitude to ensure that it makes sense. Also, the importance of using the map and compass cannot be overemphasized.

CROSSING GREENLAND

Chuck Haberbush made a one-way, unsupported trek across Greenland in 1995. He flew to Kangerlussuaq on the west coast of Greenland (see fig. 2). While there, he acquired and saved several waypoints using a GPS receiver. After meeting the other team members there, they flew to Ammassalik on the east coast of Greenland. Then their human-powered adventure began. They traveled by foot, ski, and sail for 348 miles (560 km) across the wide expanse of Greenland, using only the GPS receiver and a compass for navigation, since there were few discernable natural landmarks on which to take traditional compass bearings. Every morning they would take out the GPS receiver, let it acquire a 3-D position fix, and ask it to GO to one of the waypoints taken on Greenland's west coast. They would then set that bearing on their magnetic compass, turn off the GPS receiver, and travel following the compass bearing all morning. At their noon lunch break, they would check their bearing using the GPS receiver. The next morning they repeated the process. They did not even try to use a map; they simply followed the bearing indicated by the GPS receiver and set this bearing on their separate handheld compass. Using this technique, after five weeks, they arrived at Kangerlussuaq.

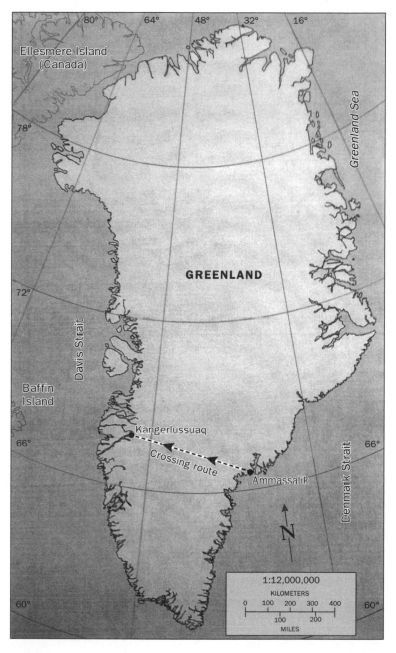

Figure 2. Greenland crossing route

Analysis: Navigation on this trip was challenging due to the importance of minimizing the weight of materials (including batteries) carried on the trek. For this reason, the GPS unit had to be used only sparingly and turned off most of the time.

CAMP MUIR, MOUNT RAINIER NATIONAL PARK

We had made the hike to Camp Muir on Mount Rainier many times, in a wide variety of conditions. This time it was a fantastic day with perfect visibility. There was no need to carry a GPS receiver for navigation, but we did so anyway, just for the fun of using it.

We started at the large parking lot at Paradise (point A in fig. 3, elevation 5450 feet). We turned on the GPS receiver, laced our boots, and applied sunscreen. After a few minutes the receiver had acquired a large number of satellites, more than enough for a solid 3-D position fix. We named the waypoint PK LOT, saved it, and turned off the receiver. After the four-hour hike, we arrived at Camp Muir (point B, elevation 10,000 feet). We turned on the receiver and let it acquire the satellites needed for a good position fix, and found the coordinates for Camp Muir on the US Geological Survey (USGS) topographic map. As expected, the coordinates we saw on the receiver's screen matched the location of Camp Muir on the map. We asked the receiver to GO to the waypoint we had named PK LOT, almost directly south of us. It told us that PK LOT was about a mile *northwest* of us, on the upper Nisqually Glacier (point C)! The position was clearly invalid, but why? After studying the map and the displayed UTM coordinates, we found that the original PK LOT coordinates were for a location about 4 miles northwest of the parking lot's correct location.

Analysis: We concluded that reflections off cars or the mountain must have produced a multipath condition that confused the receiver. This is a rare occurrence that happens when a signal from a satellite bounces off a reflective surface (such as a car or a cliff) and travels to the GPS receiver, along with the direct path signal. The reflected signal therefore gives a longer distance reading than the direct path signal and results in an erroneous position.

Never mindlessly save a waypoint without first checking the map to ensure that its location agrees with the map and common sense.

ABOUT THIS BOOK

The "wilderness" in the title of this book refers to any remote area away from civilization, roads, cell phone towers, electricity, and other modern conveniences. A person traveling in such an area usually has the objective of traveling to a specific location and returning safely to

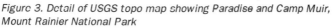

Figure 3. Detail of USGS topo map showing Paradise and Camp Muir, Mount Rainier National Park

civilization. This wilderness could be an officially designated wilderness area or any unofficial wilderness, such as the mountains, forests, desert, or a body of water.

We have made the assumption that our readers are well versed in conventional map and compass navigation and wish to expand their navigational skills by adding the GPS to their set of tools. We explain how to get the most out of your GPS receiver by using it together with a map and a compass. By studying a topographic map or chart, you can also determine if there are any features (such as mountains, cliffs, rivers, lakes, rocks, shoals, or shipping lanes) between your starting point and your objective which might not allow for safe straight-line travel as directed by the GPS receiver. Any reader who is not fully knowledgeable in the use of a conventional map and compass should read and study appendices A and B at the end of this book; they provide the minimum map and compass knowledge necessary for safe and effective GPS usage. If you do not already own a GPS receiver, we recommend that you read this book before buying one.

Finally, we wish to stress that no GPS receiver is a substitute for a conventional paper map paired with a magnetic baseplate compass. All GPS users must carry a paper map of the area in which they are traveling, as well as a conventional compass. The GPS receiver, while an extremely useful device, is not entirely foolproof, reliable, or inde-structible. It only operates as long as its batteries hold out, and it is as susceptible to failure as any other modern electronic device. No one should ever venture into the wilderness with a GPS receiver as their only navigational tool.

A NOTE ABOUT SAFETY

Safety is an important concern in all outdoor activities. No book can alert you to every hazard or anticipate the limitations of every reader. The descriptions of techniques and procedures in this book are intended to provide general information. This is not a complete text on Global Positioning System techniques. Nothing substitutes for formal instruction, routine practice, and plenty of experience. When you follow any of the procedures described here, you assume responsibility for your own safety. Use this book as a general guide to further information.

—*Mountaineers Books*

Understanding the Global Positioning System

WHAT IT IS

The Global Positioning System (GPS) is a network of satellites, ground control and communications equipment, and a very large number of users and receivers. It was originally developed by the U.S. Department of Defense for military purposes, and in the 1980s it was expanded to include civilian users. Since that time, additional enhancements and improvements to the system have made it even more accurate and useful. GPS receivers are now used by many businesses, governments, surveyors, farmers, geologists, and recreationalists. Additionally, GPS receivers are now contained in many automobiles, cell phones, sports watches, and other devices.

One of the largest groups of users to benefit from the GPS consists of hikers, scramblers, climbers, kayakers, and those involved in other recreational activities. These people can use the GPS receiver to pinpoint their position, determine the correct route to get to some other identifiable location, and use it to travel from one point to another. This group of GPS users usually relies on handheld, battery-powered GPS receivers carried in a pack or pocket. They want their receivers to be small, lightweight, easy to use, and energy efficient, which is the type this book focuses on.

THE THREE SEGMENTS

The **Space Segment** (fig. 4) nominally consists of twenty-eight satellites (such as that shown in fig. 5) circling the Earth. Since satellites occasionally fail and must be replaced, there are always a few extra satellites that can be brought online in the event of a failure and can operate before it becomes convenient to launch a new one. These satellites receive control signals transmitted from Earth and send positioning data back to the receivers on Earth.

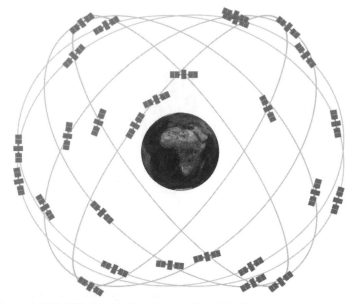

Figure 4. Global Positioning System satellite orbits (Courtesy of www.gps.gov)

Figure 5. Typical GPS satellite
(Courtesy of www.gps.gov)

The **Control Segment** (see fig. 6) is maintained by the U.S. Air Force and consists of multiple installations worldwide containing computers, communications equipment, and antennas. The Master Control Station is located at Schriever Air Force Base, near Colorado Springs, Colorado. Ground antennas and tracking and monitor stations around the world enable ground-based control personnel to make modifications and refinements to the space segment and keep the system running smoothly and accurately.

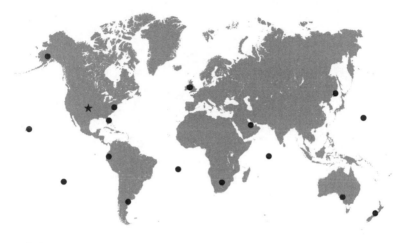

★ Colorado headquarters
● Control segment stations and antennas

Figure 6. The control segment, consisting of multiple installations worldwide
(Courtesy of www.gps.gov)

The **User Segment** consists of all of the individuals, businesses, governmental and educational institutions, and others who wish to make use of the system. When you purchase and use a GPS receiver, such as those shown in figure 7 (see page 22), you become a part of the user segment.

HOW THE GPS WORKS

The basic principle of GPS operation is based on the speed of radio signals traveling from the satellite to the user. If a GPS receiver can detect and lock onto the signal from any satellite, it can measure time with a great deal of accuracy.

Figure 7. GPS receivers for use in the wilderness

Once the signal from one satellite is detected, the receiver has the capability to precisely measure the time it takes for a signal to get from any other satellite to the user. If it acquires a second signal, it can locate the user's position as somewhere on the surface of a sphere with a radius equal to the distance to that satellite. If the receiver detects and locks onto a third satellite, it can calculate the distance to that satellite as well. The user's position can be narrowed down to the intersection of these two spheres, which is somewhere on the circumference of a circle. Finally, if a fourth satellite is detected, the user's position can be calculated to be at the intersection of that circle with a sphere whose radius is equal to the distance to the fourth satellite. This intersection only occurs at two specific places. If the receiver knows only its rough, general location (such as in North America or Africa), it can discard the incorrect location and determine the correct one.

Four satellite signals are necessary to obtain what is called a 3-D position fix, meaning that your position is known in three dimensions: latitude, longitude, and altitude. If only three satellites are acquired, the receiver knows your location to be somewhere on the circumference of a circle. Under these circumstances most GPS receivers will make the usually reasonable assumption that you are on the surface of the Earth, and your position is calculated to be the intersection of the circle with the surface of the Earth. This is called a 2-D position fix, since no altitude can be found. However, the accuracy of the horizontal position under this condition is also degraded from that found using a 3-D position fix, which explains the large position error experienced in the Chiwawa River example described in the introduction.

GPS ACCURACY
Historical Accuracy
When the GPS was originally developed, some government officials feared that it could be used against us by our perceived enemies. For this reason, they purposely degraded its accuracy through a process called selective availability, which degraded accuracy to approximately 100 meters, that is, to a sphere with a radius roughly the size of a football field. But during the 1990s, many individuals, corporations, farmers, ranchers, scientists, sportspersons, and others found the GPS to be very useful, and they realized that it could be even more useful if it were allowed to be as accurate as it potentially could be. On May 1, 2000, the Department of Defense ceased the use of selective availability, thus improving the accuracy of the GPS to a sphere with a radius roughly the size of a racquetball court.

Present Accuracy

Today, under ideal conditions, GPS position is accurate to approximately 5 meters (15 feet) most of the time. Since there are so many variables involved in GPS reception, accuracy is usually stated by GPS receiver manufacturers in probabilistic terms, such as 5 meters 95 percent of the time, and 15 meters (50 feet) 99 percent of the time.

Accuracy Enhancements and Other Satellite Systems

A refinement of GPS positioning called the Wide Area Augmentation System (WAAS) was deployed to aid aircraft but can be used by GPS receivers said to be WAAS-enabled, which means they are able to pick up a signal from either of two extra satellites permanently positioned above the equator. WAAS makes a GPS receiver more accurate. Ground-based installations receive signals from satellites and calculate a position. They compare this calculated position to the actual location, which is precisely known, and find the amount of error. Then they provide a correction to all positions based on this error. When shopping for a GPS receiver, you should look for *WAAS* on the box or in the receiver's technical specifications.

When WAAS signals are received, GPS accuracy can be as good as 3 meters (10 feet) 95 percent of the time, and 7 meters (20 feet) 99 percent of the time. This degree of accuracy can enable you to not only find the parking lot but sometimes even the exact location of your car in that lot. One problem with WAAS in the continental United States is that both WAAS satellites are quite low in the sky and their signals may be blocked by topography. The increased accuracy provided by WAAS is therefore not achievable in many locations. When using a WAAS-enabled receiver in such locations, the added accuracy due to the WAAS satellites might very well be nonexistent. Certain conditions such as heavy forest cover, canyons and gullies, signal reflections, and other situations can also degrade basic GPS accuracy.

Similar satellite systems are located in other parts of the world, including the European Geostationary Navigation Overlay System (EGNOS). The combination of WAAS and EGNOS is called the Space-Based Augmentation System (SBAS). The Russian Federation has developed a system called GLONASS *(Globalnaya navigatsionnaya sputnikovaya sistema)*. China and the European Union are also developing systems. Some GPS receivers can now access the US and Russian systems and will eventually have access to Chinese and European ones as well. With more satellites and more frequencies, users have better accuracy and more dependable operation.

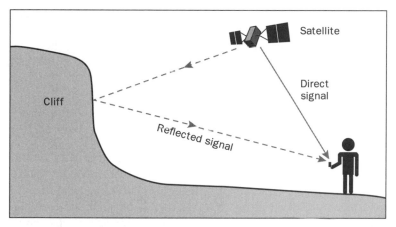

Figure 8. Multipath signal reflection

Accuracy Problems

Occasionally, certain conditions exist that degrade GPS accuracy. Though these are rare, it is important to acknowledge that they do occur. These conditions include deep canyons or heavy forest cover, in which most satellites are masked from view. In such situations, it may be impossible to obtain a decent position fix. Another problem is multipath signal reflection, in which a signal from a satellite is reflected off a rock face or a human-made object, such as a building or a vehicle (see fig. 8). The result can then be an erroneous position, as explained in the Camp Muir story in the introduction. You can easily deal with these conditions by observing the receiver's stated position and considering whether it makes sense to you, rather than just mindlessly saving the position as a waypoint.

Another accuracy problem is with the first position fix after powering up the unit. Sometimes this position is in error by up to a hundred meters or more since it is calculating position based on very few satellites, even though it may have acquired four satellites. Waiting a few minutes and observing the position readout until it stabilizes into a good 3-D position fix avoids this problem. Again, observe the displayed position, compare it to the map, and ask yourself if it makes sense before saving it.

WHAT THE GPS CAN DO FOR YOU

The single most important task for a GPS receiver is to tell you your precise geographical location, referred to as your point position. If you know your location with certainty, it is possible to find out the distance and direction to any other place shown on a map or the distance and direction to any other previously defined waypoint, whether shown on the map or not. Once you know the correct direction of travel, you can go to that intended destination using either a conventional compass (as explained in appendix B) or a compass (if any) that is part of the GPS receiver. By studying a topographic map (see appendix A), you should be able to find a feasible route from your present location to the desired objective. These are basic GPS receiver features. Any GPS receiver, regardless of cost or complexity, can be used to navigate in this manner. Beyond these features, more expensive receivers contain additional functions, such as a barometric altimeter, an electronic compass, and the ability to preload or upload topographic maps onto the receiver and to exchange waypoints and routes between the GPS receiver and a personal computer.

Selecting and Purchasing a GPS Receiver

Why do you want to own a GPS receiver at all? What do you intend to do with it? How do you intend to use it? What do you expect it to do for you? How much are you willing to pay for it? After answering these questions, you should be able to identify the level of device to purchase: basic, intermediate, or advanced.

BASIC GPS RECEIVERS

The key to identifying a basic-level receiver is to look at its advertised features, its specifications, or the information printed on the exterior of its package. The lack of a *topographic* map viewing feature, expandable memory, or preloaded or uploadable topographic maps will identify such a unit.

Most basic units do not have a built-in compass, so it is essential to carry a separate baseplate compass. Some basic receivers have preloaded road maps or "base maps" that identify major roads and streets (see fig. 9), but they do not contain topographic maps or marine charts. The ability of a receiver to

Figure 9. Typical base map displayed on a Garmin eTrex 20 GPS receiver

Table 1. Basic GPS Receivers

Brand & Model	Cost (US $)	Operating System*	Routes	Waypoints	Expandable Memory	Weight (oz)	Screen Size (diagonal in)	Color Screen	Touch Screen	Batteries	Battery Life (hrs)	Visual Map Display	Wireless Transfer	Preloaded Topo Maps	Downloadable Topos	Dimensions (in)	Minimum Temp (°F)	Maximum Temp (°F)	Compass	Altimeter	Camera
Bushnell BackTrack	60	N/A	0	3	No	1.5	1.5	No	No	2 AAA	20	No	No	No	No	4.1 x 2.8 x 0.9	5	140	Yes	No	No
Brunton GET-BACK	99	N/A	0	3	No	1.3	1.1	No	No	Special	13	No	No	No	No	2.8 x 1.5 x 0.5	5	140	Yes	No	No
Garmin eTrex 10	115	W	50	1000	No	5	2.2	No	No	2 AA	25	Yes	No	No	No	3.9 x 2.2 x 1.3	-4	158	No	No	No
Magellan eXplorist 110	130	W	25	500	No	5.2	2.2	Yes	No	2 AA	18	Yes	No	No	No	4.4 x 2.2 x 1.4	14	140	No	No	No
Garmin GPS 72H	150	W, M	500	500	No	7.7	2.7	No	No	2 AA	16	No	No	No	No	6.2 x 2.7 x 1.2	5	140	No	No	No
Magellan eXplorist GC	150	W	0	500	No	5.2	2.2	Yes	No	2 AA	18	Yes	No	No	No	4.4 x 2.2 x 1.4	14	140	No	No	No
Garmin Foretrex 301	150	W, M	20	500	No	2.3	1.7	No	No	2 AAA	15	No	No	No	No	2.9 x 1.7 x 0.9	-4	140	No	No	No
Garmin Foretrex 401	175	W, M	20	500	No	2.3	1.7	No	No	2 AA	15	No	Yes	No	No	2.9 x 1.7 x 0.9	-4	140	Yes	Yes	No
Garmin fēnix	400	W, M	50	1000	No	2.9	1.2	No	No	Li Ion	50	No	Yes	No	No	1.9 x 1.9 x 0.7	-4	122	Yes	Yes	No
Suunto Ambit	500	W, M	25	100	No	2.8	1.3	No	No	Li Ion	50	No	Yes	No	No	1.9 x 1.9 x 0.7	-5	140	Yes	Yes	No

*N/A: Cannot interface with computer. W: Windows. M: Macintosh (Apple).

display detailed topographic maps is not an essential element of GPS usage since you can observe the coordinates displayed on a GPS receiver and then find the corresponding location on a paper map using UTM or the latitude/longitude grid. Since we expect you to carry a paper map, having the topo map displayed on the screen is somewhat redundant and more of a convenience than an absolute requirement.

A selection of some of these basic-level GPS receivers is given in table 1, along with their features. Most cost less than two hundred dollars and provide a location in three dimensions, that is, north–south, east–west, and altitude. A barometric altimeter is therefore not necessary for the determination of altitude with a GPS receiver.

A few extremely simple and inexpensive GPS devices are on the market, including the Bushnell BackTrack (see fig. 10) and the Brunton GET-BACK. These are not fully functional GPS receivers in the sense that they tell you exactly where you are. Instead, they tell you how to get *back* to a location where you previously were, and where you had created a waypoint. If all you want to do is return to your home, your car, or your camp, these devices are ideal, since they are inexpensive (under a hundred dollars) and very easy to use. But if

Figure 10. The Bushnell BackTrack GPS device

you want to identify your exact point position, store more than a very few waypoints, or go to a location you have never been to, neither of these two receivers will work for you. Receivers like these do not display your map coordinates, so they will not give you your point position.

Some receivers, such as Garmin's Foretrex and fēnix and Suunto's Ambit, are wrist-mounted units made for outdoor activities requiring both hands, such as kayaking and skiing. They do not display your position on a map, but they do give you position coordinates, which you can pinpoint on your paper map and navigate to a previously saved destination.

Most GPS receivers can be used with a home computer from which you can download waypoints onto the receiver or upload GPS data to the computer. Sometimes GPS software updates are also available online from the manufacturer, and these can then be loaded onto the receiver.

The connection is usually made with a cable that plugs into a USB port on the computer. The Operating System column in tables 1, 2, and 3 indicates this capability. If you wish to make use of this capability (though it is not necessary for basic orientation and navigation purposes), it is important to make sure it is compatible with your computer.

INTERMEDIATE GPS RECEIVERS

Intermediate GPS receivers contain all the features of the basic units but include an important feature: the ability to display detailed topographic maps. Some receivers (such as the DeLorme Earthmate PN-60 and the Magellan 610 and 710) come preloaded with detailed topographic maps comparable to USGS 7.5-minute, 1:24,000-scale topo maps, or they come with CDs containing such maps. For others (such as many Garmin models and the Magellan eXplorist 310 and 510), you can purchase digital topographic maps at an added cost and upload them to the GPS receiver. An example of a topographic map display is shown in figure 11.

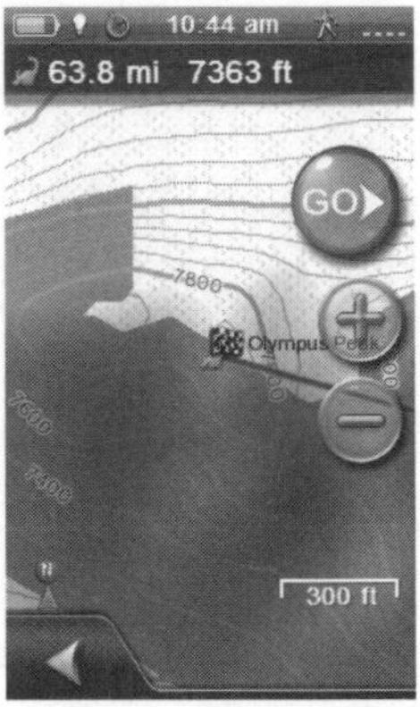

Figure 11. Typical topographic map displayed on a Magellan eXplorist 610 GPS receiver

When the intermediate-level receiver identifies its location, it can show that position on the detailed topographic map. As you move, the position is continually updated on the electronic map. Later, at home, you can download the route and the waypoints onto your computer. If the receiver is turned off when not in use, the waypoints taken will be plotted on the map. If the receiver is kept on, however, the entire trip (called a "track") will be shown on the topo map. This method of operation will drain the batteries much more quickly that the sporadic use of the receiver, so it will be essential to carry a sufficient number of spare batteries if you choose to do this.

An intermediate receiver can also accept SD or micro-SD cards (see fig. 12), such as Garmin's TOPO US 24K Topocards, which contain 1:24,000-scale topo maps. USGS topographic maps for a large state or several smaller states can be purchased separately for about eighty to a hundred dollars each. These can be used with a variety of Garmin receivers. Magellan receivers can make use of similar cards with slightly different topo maps that cost about fifty dollars for each geographic region. Some Magellan receivers (such as the eXplorist 610 and 710)

Table 2. Intermediate GPS Receivers

Brand & Model	Cost (US $)	Operating System*	Routes**	Waypoints**	Expandable Memory	Weight (oz)	Screen Size (diagonal in)	Color Screen	Touch Screen	Batteries	Battery Life (hrs)	Wireless Transfer	Preloaded Topo Maps	Downloadable Topos	Dimensions (in)	Minimum Temp (°F)	Maximum Temp (°F)	Compass	Altimeter	Camera
Magellan eXplorist 310	180	W	50	1000	No	5.2	2.2	Yes	No	2AA	18	No		Yes	4.4 x 2.2 x 1.4	14	140	No	No	No
Garmin eTrex 20	185	W, M	200	2000	Yes	5	2.2	Yes	No	2AA	25	No	Base	Yes	4.0 x 2.1 x 1.3	-4	158	No	No	No
Garmin Dakota 10	200	W, M	50	1000	Yes	5.5	2.6	Yes	Yes	2AA	20	No	Base	Yes	3.9 x 2.2 x 1.3	5	158	No	No	No
Garmin GPS MAP 78	250	W, M	2000	2000	Yes	7.7	2.6	Yes	No	2AA	20	No	Base	Yes	6.0 x 2.6 x 1.2	5	158	No	No	No
Garmin eTrex 30	280	W, M	200	2000	Yes	5	2.2	Yes	No	2AA	25	Yes	Base	Yes	4.0 x 2.1 x 1.3	-4	158	Yes	Yes	No
Garmin Dakota 20	280	W, M	50	1000	Yes	5.5	2.6	Yes	Yes	2AA	20	Yes	Base	Yes	3.9 x 2.2 x 1.3	5	158	Yes	Yes	No
Magellan eXplorist 510	280	W	200	2000	Yes	6.9	3.0	Yes	Yes	2AA	16	No	Base	Yes	5.0 x 2.6 x 1.5	14	140	No	No	3.2 MP
Garmin Oregon 450	300	W, M	200	1000	Yes	6.8	3.0	Yes	Yes	2AA	16	Yes	Base	Yes	4.5 x 2.3 x 1.4	-4	158	Yes	Yes	No
Garmin GPSMAP 62	300	W, M	200	2000	No	9.2	2.6	Yes	No	2AA	20	No	Base	Yes	6.3 x 2.4 x 1.4	5	158	No	No	No
DeLorme Earthmate PN-60	300	W	Var	Var	Yes	5.3	2.2	Yes	No	2AA	14	No	24K	Yes	5.3 x 2.4 x 1.5	-4	167	Yes	Yes	No

*W: Windows. M: Macintosh (Apple). **Var: Variable number

Table 2. Intermediate GPS Receivers continued

Brand & Model	Cost (US $)	Operating System*	Routes**	Waypoints**	Expandable Memory	Weight (oz)	Screen Size (diagonal in)	Color Screen	Touch Screen	Batteries	Battery Life (hrs)	Wireless Transfer	Preloaded Topo Maps	Downloadable Topos	Dimensions (in)	Minimum Temp (°F)	Maximum Temp (°F)	Compass	Altimeter	Camera
DeLorme Earthmate PN-60W	350	W	100	1500	Yes	5.3	2.2	Yes	No	2AA	14	Yes	24K	Yes	5.3 x 2.4 x 1.5	-4	167	Yes	Yes	No
Garmin GPS MAP 78s	350	W, M	2000	2000	Yes	7.7	2.6	Yes	No	2AA	20	Yes	Base	Yes	6.0 x 2.6 x 1.2	5	158	Yes	Yes	No
Garmin Rino 610	350	W, M	2000	2000	Yes	6.8	3.0	Yes	Yes	2AA	16	Yes	Base	Yes	4.5 x 2.3 x 1.4	-4	140	Yes	Yes	No
Garmin Oregon 450t	365	W, M	200	1000	Yes	6.8	3.0	Yes	Yes	2AA	16	Yes	100K	Yes	4.5 x 2.3 x 1.4	-4	158	Yes	Yes	No
Garmin GPSMAP 62s	390	W, M	200	2000	Yes	9.2	2.6	Yes	No	2AA	20	Yes	Base	Yes	6.3 x 2.4 x 1.4	5	158	Yes	Yes	No
Magellan eXplorist 610	400	W	200	2000	Yes	6.9	3.0	Yes	Yes	2AA	16	No	24K	Yes	5.0 x 2.6 x 1.5	14	140	Yes	Yes	3.2 MP
Garmin Oregon 550	400	W, M	200	2000	Yes	6.8	3.0	Yes	Yes	2AA	16	Yes	Base	Yes	4.5 x 2.3 x 1.4	-4	158	Yes	Yes	Yes

*W: Windows. M: Macintosh (Apple). **Var: Variable number

come with preloaded maps called the
Summit Series, which contain 1:24,000-
scale maps. The two DeLorme receivers
come with CDs containing maps covering the entire United States, Canada,
and Mexico. Yet another variation is a
subscription service for thirty to forty
dollars a year (such as DeLorme's), which

*Figure 12. Micro-SD card
compared to a dime*

allows you to download additional USGS topographic maps, marine
charts, and other specialized materials.

A large number of GPS receivers are intermediate level, and many are
listed in table 2. Their costs range from less than two hundred dollars
to four hundred dollars, depending on their features.

Many Garmin receivers come with preloaded 1:100,000-scale maps;
this feature is indicated by the letter "t" in their model numbers. The
1:100,000-scale topo maps are far less detailed than the 1:24,000-scale
topo maps and are adequate for trail hiking but not detailed enough for
off-trail activities.

Many intermediate-level receivers also contain built-in compasses, so
theoretically you could discard your paper maps and baseplate compass
and do all your wilderness navigating with this level of GPS receiver
alone. But it's not recommended to rely solely on the GPS receiver,
since batteries can die, you could lose or damage it, or it could fail for
some other reason. It is also inconvenient and time-consuming to be
frequently panning the GPS unit to get to the portion of the map you
want to see, then zooming in to see it in detail. This sort of map usage
also requires a lot of battery power, and the small screen size (usually 3
inches or smaller) severely limits the amount of visibility. A paper map
can be folded up to show your route, and you can stuff it into your
pocket and whip it out any time you want to refer to it. Preloaded and
downloaded maps displayed on a 3-inch screen are no substitute for a
convenient paper map.

ADVANCED GPS RECEIVERS

Some GPS receivers contain even more features than the intermediate-level receivers (see table 3). Garmin's Rino series allows voice
communication and is particularly suited to search-and-rescue operations. Some receivers have digital cameras, and some allow digital data
transfer, such as route and waypoint data communication, between two
or more GPS receivers. These receivers generally cost more than four
hundred dollars, though the cost of the maps is not included for all.

Table 3. Advanced GPS Receivers

Brand & Model	Cost (US $)	Operating System*	Routes	Waypoints	Expandable Memory	Weight (oz)	Screen Size (diagonal in)	Color Screen	Touch Screen	Batteries	Battery Life (hrs)	Wireless Transfer	Preloaded Topo Maps	Downloadable Topos	Dimensions (in)	Minimum Temp (°F)	Maximum Temp (°F)	Compass	Altimeter	Camera
Garmin GPSMAP 78sc	450	W, M	2000	2000	Yes	7.7	2.6	Yes	No	2 AA	20	Yes	Marine	Yes	6 x 2.6 x 1.2	5	158	Yes	Yes	No
Garmin GPSMAP 62sc	460	W, M	200	2000	Yes	7.5	2.6	Yes	No	2 AA	15	No	Base	Yes	6.3 x 2.4 x 1.4	5	158	Yes	Yes	5 MP
Garmin GPSMAP 62st	475	W, M	200	2000	Yes	9.2	2.6	Yes	No	2 AA	20	Yes	100K	Yes	6.3 x 2.4 x 1.4	5	158	Yes	Yes	No
Garmin Oregon 550t	500	W, M	200	2000	Yes	6.8	3	Yes	Yes	2 AA	16	Yes	100K	Yes	4.5 x 2.3 x 1.4	-4	158	Yes	Yes	3.2 MP
Garmin Rino 650	500	W, M	2000	2000	Yes	11.3	2.6	Yes	No	2AA	18	Yes	Base	Yes	7.5 x 2.4 x 2.2	-4	140	No	No	No
Magellan eXplorist 710	500	W	200	2000	Yes	6.9	3	Yes	Yes	2 AA	16	No	24K**	Yes	5.0 x 2.6 x 1.5	14	140	Yes	Yes	3.2 MP
Garmin Montana 600	515	W, M	200	2000	Yes	11.7	4	Yes	Yes	2 AA	16	Yes	Base	Yes	5.7 x 2.9 x 1.4	-4	158	Yes	Yes	No
Garmin GPSMAP 62stc	530	W, M	200	2000	Yes	7.5	2.6	Yes	No	2 AA	15	Yes	100K	Yes	6.3 x 2.4 x 1.4	5	158	Yes	Yes	5 MP
Garmin Montana 650	550	W, M	200	2000	Yes	11.7	4	Yes	Yes	Li Ion	16	Yes	100K	Yes	5.7 x 2.9 x 1.4	-4	158	Yes	Yes	5 MP
Garmin Rino 655t	550	W, M	200	2000	Yes	11.3	2.6	Yes	Yes	Li Ion	14	Yes	100K	Yes	7.5 x 2.4 x 2.2	-4	140	Yes	Yes	5 MP
Garmin Montana 650t	600	W, M	200	2000	Yes	11.7	4	Yes	Yes	Li Ion	16	Yes	100K	Yes	5.7 x 2.9 x 1.4	-4	158	Yes	Yes	5 MP

*W: Windows. M: Macintosh (Apple). **Includes City Series USA road maps.

If cost is no object, you might want to get a receiver with an electronic compass, a barometric altimeter, and other added features. But if cost is an important consideration, we recommend skipping these features, since you should always carry an ordinary baseplate compass, and wearing an altimeter watch is always a good idea if traveling in mountainous terrain, since it can provide you with a good estimate of your altitude without draining the batteries of your GPS receiver. You also need to be aware of the fact that some electronic compasses in GPS receivers easily lose their calibration if the unit is bumped, if you change batteries, or for no apparent reason, making it necessary to recalibrate often. An electronic compass within a GPS receiver is no substitute for a simple baseplate compass (see appendix B.)

GPS RECEIVER SERIES

Our intent here is to help you be a more informed buyer by providing the characteristics of each of several different families of receivers. We do not endorse any particular brand or type of unit. They all work.

DeLorme

DeLorme, a well-known producer of maps, also produces the Earthmate series of GPS receivers. There are two models, the PN-60 and the PN-60w (fig. 13), each with a 2.2-inch screen. The main difference between these two devices is that the PN-60w model has wireless communication capability with the inReach unit (at an additional cost of about $250), which allows for text satellite communication even when you are out of range of cell phone towers. Otherwise, both contain altimeters and compasses and come with CDs containing 1:24,000-scale maps for all of North America.

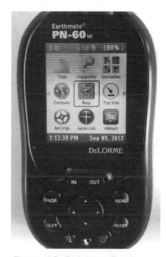

Figure 13. DeLorme Earthmate PN-60w GPS device

Garmin

Garmin has the largest selection of GPS receivers. These are divided into various series, some better suited to certain activities than others.

The **Montana** series has the largest screen size at 4 inches and is particularly suited to use in a vehicle. The display is dual-orientation (landscape or portrait) and has a touch screen. It is also the heaviest of receivers, weighing in at nearly twelve ounces, so hikers and back-packers who wish to minimize the weight they carry might consider a different unit, though this family of receivers will give the best map detail. The least expensive unit includes a compass and an altimeter and accepts Garmin 1:24,000-scale maps at an added cost. The next higher-priced unit adds a 5 MP camera, and the most expensive unit is preloaded with 1:100,000-scale maps.

The **GPSMAP 62** series receivers all have a quad-helix antenna, which may sometimes give better reception in challenging topography or under heavy forest cover. The least expensive unit comes with a 2.6-inch color screen. More expensive units are described with suffixes of "s" (for sensors) for electronic compass and altimeter, "c" for 5 MP camera, and "t" for preloaded 1:100,000-scale topo maps. At about nine ounces, they are intermediate in weight between the Montana and the smaller units.

The **Oregon** series receivers are smaller than the GPSMAP 62, and all have a 3-inch touch-screen display. They weigh about seven ounces, and each unit in the series has a compass and an altimeter. More expensive receivers in this family add preloaded 1:000,000-scale maps, a 3.2 MP camera, and wireless data transfer.

The **Dakota** series receivers are smaller and lighter than those described above but still has a 2.6-inch color touch-screen display. At about six ounces, they are more attractive to hikers and backpackers, but maps must be purchased separately for each version. The least expensive Dakota has no compass or altimeter; the more expensive unit has both. Neither has a camera.

The **eTrex** series receivers are the lightest of the handheld Garmin units and very popular with hikers and back-packers. The basic Model 10, with a 2.2-inch monochrome screen, is inexpensive, but it cannot accept or display topo maps and does not have a compass or altimeter. The Model 20 (fig. 14) has a 2.2-inch color display, plus the capability to display topo maps (purchased separately); the Model 30 adds a compass, an altimeter, and wireless connectivity.

*Figure 14. Garmin eTrex
20 GPS device*

The **GPS 72** and **78** series receivers are particularly suited to maritime activities since they are waterproof and they float if dropped into the water. At about eight ounces, they are midweight compared to the Montana and the eTrex units. The basic GPS 72H is quite inexpensive, has a 2.2-inch monochrome display, and does not accept maps. More expensive units in this family add 2.6-inch color screens, compass and altimeter, micro-SD card slots to support topo maps and marine charts, wireless connectivity, and preloaded US marine charts.

The **Foretrex** series consists of two models, the 301 and the 401. They are very similar except that the 401 has a compass and altimeter while the 301 does not. Both are wrist-worn, have 1.7-inch monochrome screens, and weigh approximately two ounces. Neither supports downloading or viewing topographic maps. These are particularly suited to activities requiring both hands, such as skiing and paddling.

The **Rino** series of Garmin devices feature FRS/GMRS (Family Radio Service/General Mobile Radio Service) radio communication as well as GPS functions. All have 2.6-inch color touch screens, and their radio range is either up to 5 miles or up to 20 miles, depending on the model. These are best suited to search-and-rescue and similar purposes. Their weight (eleven to twelve ounces) might be excessive to the weight-conscious hiker.

Magellan

Magellan has a series of GPS receivers known as the eXplorist family. Ranging from five to seven ounces, they are small enough for hiking and backpacking, yet provide a wide choice of features. The eXplorist GC is optimized for geocaching, but not for hiking or other wilderness purposes, since it does not allow the creation and use of routes. A better choice is the less expensive Model 110, with a 2.2-inch color screen but no map capability, or the Model 310, which accepts 1:24,000-scale maps (at an added cost). The Model 510 adds a 3-inch touch screen and a 3.2 MP camera, and the Model 610 (fig. 15) adds preloaded Summit Series 1:24,000-scale topographic maps for either the entire

Figure 15. Magellan eXplorist 610 GPS device

United States or for all of Canada at no additional cost. The Model 710 adds preloaded City Series maps, which provide turn-by-turn driving directions, as well as all the features found on the Model 610.

WHAT TO LOOK FOR WHEN SELECTING A GPS RECEIVER

With such a wide variety of GPS units on the market, it is important for you to weigh some important factors before purchasing a unit. First, ensure that the unit does all the things that you want it to. Is computer connectivity important to you? How about weight and battery life? Do you want to be able to use the same batteries as in another device you will be carrying? Consider the desirability of a touch screen, a joystick, a camera, the maximum number of routes and waypoints, ability to accept and display maps, electronic compass, and certainly price. If you intend to use the device frequently, and are willing to spend considerable time in learning how to use it and practicing its use, it may make sense to spend a lot and get a top-of-the-line unit. On the other hand, if you plan on using it only occasionally, you may decide to get a more modest unit.

Coordinate Systems

On USGS 7.5-minute topographic maps (the type most widely used by wilderness travelers), latitude is identified only every 2.5 minutes, which corresponds to approximately every 3 miles (5 km). Longitude is identified about every 2 miles (3 km), which makes it difficult to identify a precise point position on USGS topo maps using the lat/long coordinate system.

The Universal Transverse Mercator (UTM) coordinate system is a more precise way of specifying position. It is based on a grid of north–south and east–west lines spaced exactly 1 km (0.6214 mile) apart. The edges of USGS topo maps contain small numbers identifying each of these lines, allowing you to find your location quickly and easily to an accuracy of roughly 100 meters (about 100 yards). Most GPS receivers allow you to use the UTM system instead of (or in addition to) the latitude/longitude system. You will need to learn the UTM system in order to use your basic-level GPS receiver most effectively.

If reading the description of UTM makes you feel uncomfortable about your abilities to use it (perhaps due to its use of the metric system), then we recommend that you pay a little more to get a receiver with detailed topographic map display capability, as listed in tables 2 and 3. Such receivers can display your point position on a screen with a detailed topo map, thus making it unnecessary for you to calculate or interpret the UTM coordinates.

If you feel entirely comfortable with the UTM system, and if afford-ability is an important consideration in your choice, consider one of the basic units described in table 1.

Battery Life and Types

Battery life is an important consideration in selecting a GPS receiver. Advertised battery life ranges from twelve hours to twenty-five hours, but the actual battery life you experience may be less, depending on how you use the receiver (particularly using backlight or maps). If you intend to do most of your wilderness adventures with the receiver turned on all the time, a twelve-hour advertised life might not be enough for a day's trip, and you should carry at least one additional set of batteries. Selecting a receiver with a twenty-five-hour battery life should allow you to keep the receiver on all day without carrying extra batteries. This is particularly important for trips on which you try to limit unnecessary weight.

Another consideration is the type of batteries required for the receiver: standard AA or AAA, or proprietary batteries. It is easy to find standard-sized batteries at most convenience stores and gas sta-tions along the way to your wilderness destination, but it is difficult to find special proprietary batteries. Most receivers allow use of standard AA or AAA cells, which are available in a variety of forms, including rechargeable batteries. If you plan on using your GPS unit a lot, you can save money in the long run by investing in a set or two of rechargeable batteries and a charging unit. Lithium batteries usually have the longest life, though they are more expensive than alkaline batteries. Lithium cells are also better under cold-temperature operation. Battery compat-ibility with other devices, such as your digital camera, headlamp, and MP3 player should also be considered.

Cold-Temperature Operation

The lower operating temperature of available GPS receivers ranges from -4 degrees F (-20 degrees C) to 14 degrees F (-10 degrees C). This is important if you plan on using your receiver while ice fishing or snow-mobiling in northern states, climbing Mount McKinley, or exploring in the Arctic or Antarctic. In temperatures below the minimum specified operating temperature, the liquid-crystal display (LCD) can go blank, rendering GPS usage impossible. Be sure the device you purchase will work in the temperatures that you expect to encounter.

Another consideration when selecting a GPS receiver for cold-temperature use is to examine the size and locations of the operating buttons, including touch-screen operation, and determine whether you will be able to operate it while wearing gloves or mittens. Is it water-proof or at least water resistant, so that you can use it in rain, sleet, or snow?

GPS Manufacturers' Websites

Manufacturers' websites such as www.magellangps.com, www.garmin.com, www.delorme.com, www.lowrance.com, and www.brunton.com can assist you in making an informed choice. These sites provide device specifications and often contain complete owner's manuals from which you can obtain important information relating to the receiver's capabilities and limitations. Most manufacturers only supply quick start guides with their units and refer purchasers to their website for the complete owner's manual. Reading an owner's manual online before purchasing a certain receiver can give you valuable insight into its operation, helping you to make a more informed decision as to whether to buy that unit.

Other Sources of Information

Before making a final decision as to which receiver to buy, it is a good idea to check independent online product reviews on sites such as www.amazon.com, www.rei.com, www.bestbuy.com, www.thegpsstore.com, and www.outdoorgearlab.com. You can also do an internet search for handheld GPS reviews. These reviews also contain useful insights into unit strengths and weaknesses, reliability, battery life, accuracy, customer service, and warranty/return policies.

GPS LEARNING CURVE

It is important to remember that the more things an electronic device can do, the more difficult it is to learn how to use all the features you paid for. If your main motivation is to avoid getting lost and to be able to get back to civilization if you ever do get lost, then perhaps it might be wise to begin your GPS usage with a very simple, basic-level device such as a Garmin eTrex 10 or a Magellan eXplorist 110. Later, if you wish to graduate to a more complex device with expanded capabilities, you could give your basic receiver to some deserving beginner, or perhaps keep it in reserve in the event of failure of your more advanced unit.

Getting Started with Your GPS Receiver

After considerable study and reflection, you finally take the plunge and buy a GPS receiver. You should examine the contents of the box to verify that it contains all necessary materials, such as a USB cable to connect the unit to your computer, a quick start guide, and an instruction manual (or a CD or a link to an online website containing it). You need to read the instruction manual, but doing so is often boring and tedious, and you are probably itching to get it working right away. We suggest that you just read the quick start guide and get the receiver working. After gaining some basic familiarity with the unit, a thorough and careful reading of the entire instruction manual will be much more meaningful to you.

INITIAL SETUP AND FIRST POSITION FIX

Take the quick start guide and follow the instructions to install the batteries. Then continue to follow the setup instructions, turning the unit on and initializing it if necessary. Take the unit outside where there is an unobstructed view of the sky.

This chapter will explain how to perform a few of the most important and basic functions for three specific receivers from three different manufacturers, representing a variety of different screen types and user interfaces. Your receiver may be different from those described here, and therefore may have different methods for performing these operations, but the following descriptions should nevertheless be helpful for learning how to operate your receiver.

The **DeLorme Earthmate PN-60w** has a push-button panel, similar to many others with the same user interface. The basic operation of the simpler Earthmate PN-60 is nearly identical, so the following descriptions apply to both. Pressing and holding the red POWER button (see fig. 13, page 35) turns on the unit and brings up the main menu (fig. 16). In the upper left corner is the satellite status statement, initially saying NO FIX. This means that there are insufficient satellites to get a position fix.

Figure 16. DeLorme Earthmate PN-60w main menu: "Map" icon selected

Map and Satellite Screens

The main menu has a box around the center icon, labeled "Map." Pressing the down arrow button highlights the round "Satellites" icon (fig. 17), and pressing ENTER reveals the Satellite Status screen (fig. 18). If you have a clear view of much of the sky, the NO FIX in the upper left corner of the screen should eventually change to 3-D, and the status of the satellites will be shown on the screen (fig. 19). This indicates that you have acquired enough satellites for a reasonably accurate position fix. The lower left corner should display the estimated accuracy in feet (which you can change to meters later if you wish). This is only a very rough estimate of accuracy, based on the number and positions of the satellites you have acquired. The actual accuracy could be better or

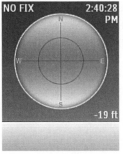

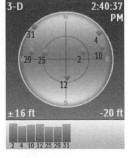

Figure 17. DeLorme main menu: "Satellites" icon selected

Figure 18. DeLorme Satellite Status screen: "NO FIX" displayed

Figure 19. DeLorme Satellite Status screen: 3-D position found

worse than that shown. If the screen suddenly goes dim, the unit has entered a built-in power save mode. Pressing the IN or OUT button will restore the screen's brightness. This first position fix might require five to ten minutes, but subsequent position fixes will be much quicker.

If the upper left corner displays 2-D, it means that you do not have enough satellites for a 3-D display. It therefore sacrifices altitude in favor of horizontal position. The altitude display (in the lower right corner of the Satellite Status screen) will therefore be frozen at whatever elevation it last recorded and will not change until you acquire enough signals for a 3-D display. You should never trust a horizontal position or an elevation with a 2-D position. Once you have a reliable 3-D position fix, pressing the QUIT button restores the main menu.

Position Coordinate System and Datum

If you plan to use your receiver with USGS topo maps, changing the coordinate system to UTM allows the display of distance in more easily recognizable units of meters (approximately 1 yard) rather than the more awkward lat/long system. To do this, use the arrows to highlight the "Settings" icon on the main menu and press ENTER to get the Settings screen. Scroll down to highlight "Units" (fig. 20). Pressing ENTER brings up the Units display of figure 21, with "Deg, Min, Sec" highlighted for "Coordinates: Primary." Pressing ENTER brings up other choices, and you can select "UTM/UPS" (Universal Transverse Mercator, for non-polar regions, and Universal Polar Stereographic, for polar regions). Press ENTER. The screen will probably also show "Datum: Primary" to be WGS-84, which is the default in most receivers but is wrong for most USGS topo maps. For USGS topo maps, it is

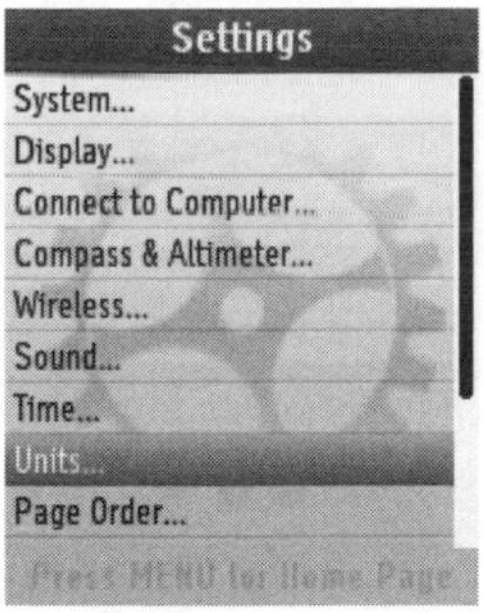

Settings	Units	Units
System...	Coordinates: Primary	Coordinates: Primary
Display...	Deg, Min, Sec	UTM/UPS
Connect to Computer...	Datum: Primary	Datum: Primary
Compass & Altimeter...	WGS84	NAD27 Continental US
Wireless...	Coordinates: Secondary	Coordinates: Secondary
Sound...	Deg, Min, Sec	Deg, Min, Sec
Time...	Datum: Secondary	Datum: Secondary
Units...	WGS84	WGS84
Page Order...	Measures	Measures
Press MENU for Home Page	Nautical Miles/Feet	Statute Miles

Figure 20. DeLorme Settings screen: "Units" selected

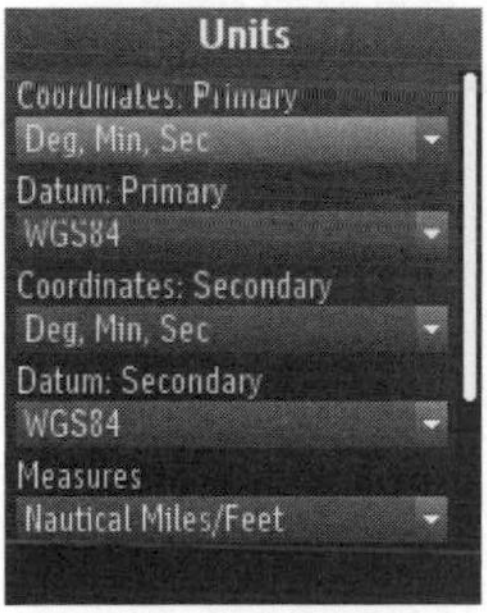

Figure 21. DeLorme Units screen: default coordinates and datum displayed

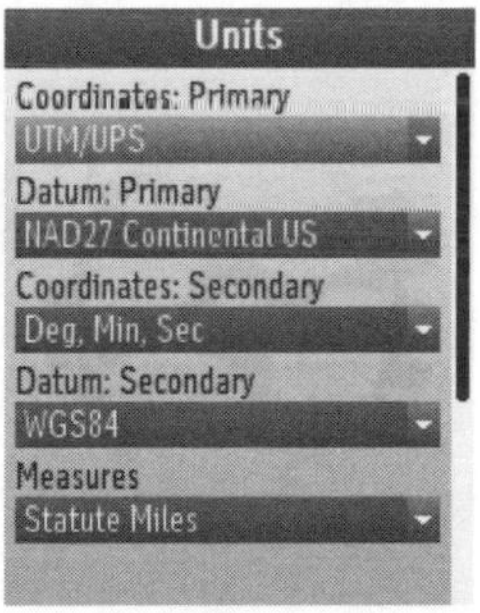

Figure 22. DeLorme Units screen: coordinates and datum changed to UTM/ UPS and NAD27

usually NAD 27 (the datum is printed on the lower left corner of USGS topo maps). If this is the case, then highlight "NAD 27 Continental US" and press ENTER to change the datum (fig. 22). If you use the wrong datum, your horizontal position as seen on the topo map can be in error by hundreds of feet or meters.

If you plan on using your GPS receiver along with marine navigation charts that show position only in lat/long, then it will be better for you to keep the default settings of lat/long for easier comparison with the marine chart. But be sure to check the datum on the chart, if it is listed, and change your GPS datum to agree if it differs.

Selecting "Units" on the Settings screen also allows you to change other units, such as compass bearings referenced to true or magnetic north. The magnetic north reference is usually preferable for use with marine navigation charts and marine compasses (see chapter 5), while true bearings are best for land navigation as seen on USGS topo maps.

Some receivers allow you to use two coordinate systems: a primary and a secondary coordinate system. If your receiver has this feature (which the Earthmate does), we suggest that you select UTM as the primary and lat/long as the secondary when using USGS topo maps. This enables you to enter and read waypoints in either system and readily convert from one system to another. If you are using marine charts, use lat/long as the primary system, and UTM as the secondary.

Marking Your Position as a Waypoint

Once your unit is set up properly, return to the Map screen by pressing QUIT twice to return to the main menu, then use the arrow buttons to

Figure 23. DeLorme Map screen: triangle indicates your position.

Figure 24. DeLorme Mark screen showing UTM coordinates and user-entered name

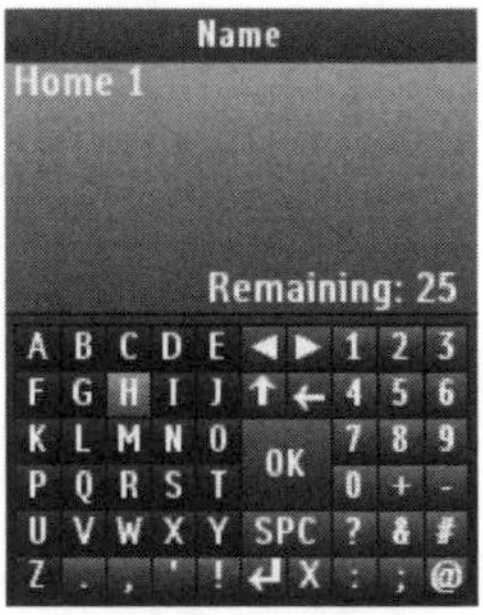

Figure 25. DeLorme alphabetic keyboard used to rename waypoint

highlight the "Map" icon, and press ENTER. Look at the map carefully (fig. 23), using the IN and OUT buttons to zoom in or out, to make sure that the unit is properly displaying your correct location (indicated by a triangle). Once you are sure of your location, press the MARK button (the button with the white pushpin symbol at the very bottom of the Earthmate; see fig. 13, page 35). This saves your current position as a waypoint and brings up the Mark screen (fig. 24). It shows the UTM coordinates and elevation of the waypoint.

The very top of the Mark screen has the name of the waypoint. If a waypoint has already been saved, it displays the name of that waypoint, followed by a number. If there is no previously saved waypoint, it will show an automatically generated name. You can use the assigned name, or you can rename the waypoint, for example, HOME. Use the up arrow to highlight the name and press ENTER, which reveals an alphabetic keyboard (fig. 25). Scroll to "H," press ENTER, then "O," ENTER, and so on to spell HOME. When you've finished typing in the name, select "OK" and press ENTER. You have now changed the name of the waypoint.

Traveling to a Waypoint

To travel to an established waypoint, go to the main menu and select the "Waypoints" icon and press ENTER. This brings up a list of all your previously saved waypoints (fig. 26). Select the waypoint you want to go to by using the down arrow to highlight the waypoint, such as Car in figure 26. The note at the bottom of the screen shows that this waypoint is 9.19 miles from your present position, at a compass bearing of 13 degrees true. You could then set the bearing of 13 degrees on your baseplate compass and travel at that bearing until you reach the car. Alternatively, you could use the GPS receiver's built-in electronic compass, by returning to the main menu and selecting the "Compass" icon.

Figure 26. DeLorme list of saved waypoints, found by selecting "Waypoints" from main menu

The **Garmin eTrex 20** GPS receiver is also representative of the eTrex 10 and 30. The eTrex series is very popular, and the instructions presented here apply with only minor variations to the other eTrex units. Other Garmin GPS families operate differently.

Thumbstick and Main Menu

Instead of DeLorme's up-down-left-right arrow buttons, the eTrex has a "thumbstick" that is used to navigate around the receiver (see fig. 14, page 36). Upon turning it on, you see the main menu (fig. 27), which contains up to twenty-four different windows, only six of which are shown at any time. Scrolling up and down with the thumbstick allows you to see the others. The last one down (or the first one up, since these wrap around) is the Satellite screen (fig. 28). Pushing the thumbstick selects the Satellite screen, where you can see the progress of the satellite acquisition process (fig. 29). If more than four satellite signals are shown, you most likely have a solid 3-D position. Though 2-D or 3-D status is not shown, you can nevertheless tell from the display how good a signal you have by observing the GPS + GLONASS accuracy and the elevation displays as well as the number of satellites acquired. If the estimated accuracy is less than 30 feet (10 meters) and if the elevation is slowly changing, you have a solid 3-D position. If the estimated accuracy is more than 30 feet, or if the elevation seems to be frozen and unchanging, you probably have an unreliable 2-D position. This screen also shows your position coordinates in the upper left corner.

  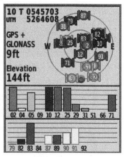

Figure 27. Garmin eTrex 20 main menu: "Map" icon selected

Figure 28. Garmin eTrex 20 main menu: "Satellite" icon selected

Figure 29. Garmin eTrex 20 Satellite screen: coordinates, accuracy, and elevation shown

Default Screen Dimming

If the screen suddenly dims, move the thumbstick left or right or up or down and the screen should return to its original brightness. It automatically dims after a preset time to save battery power. If you want to set a different time before the screen dims, press the BACK button near the upper right side of the unit to return to the main menu, scroll to Setup, then Display, and you will see a screen showing Backlight Timer. Push the thumbstick and a screen displays various times from fifteen seconds to two minutes. Select the time you prefer, push the thumbstick once and the BACK button twice to return to Setup and then the main menu.

Coordinate System, Datum, and Units

To change the coordinate system from lat/long to UTM, press the BACK button near the receiver's upper right side to return to the main menu, scroll down to the Setup window, and push the thumbstick to reveal the Setup screen. Scroll to "Position Format" (fig. 30), and push the thumbstick again. The default position format is hddd mm ss.s, meaning degrees, minutes, and seconds. Scroll through various national and regional systems until you find UTM/UPS. Press the thumbstick and the coordinate system and map datum appear, as in figure 31, which shows the usual default setting of WGS 84. You can scroll through the various datums until you find NAD 27 CONUS (for continental US), or whatever datum is shown for your topo map, and push the thumbstick.

Pressing the BACK button returns you to the Setup screen, where you can also see the Units window. Scrolling up to it and pushing the thumbstick allows you to select distances in statute or nautical miles, and elevations in feet or meters. The Setup screen also has a Heading window (fig. 32), which allows you to select either true or magnetic north reference. Select "True" for use with USGS topographic maps, or "Magnetic" for marine charts.

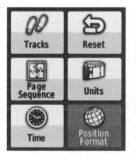

Position Format	Display
UTM UPS	**Directional Letters**
Map Datum	North Reference
Viti Levu 1916	True
Wake-Eniwetok	**Magnetic**
WGS 72	**Grid**
WGS 84	**User**
Zanderij	Go To Line (Pointer)
None	**Bearing (Large)**
User	

Figure 30. Garmin eTrex 20 Setup screen: "Position Format" selected

Figure 31. Garmin eTrex 20 Position Format screen: default WGS 84 map datum shown

Figure 32. Garmin eTrex 20 Heading screen: "True North" selected

Using the Map Screen

Once the unit is set up to your liking, press the BACK button near the upper right side of the receiver twice (once to return to Setup, another to return to the main menu). Use the thumbstick to scroll to the "Map" icon and push the thumbstick. This should show your location with a blue arrow on the map. You can use the IN and OUT buttons on the upper left side of the receiver (indicated by black up and down arrows) to zoom in and out. There should also be a white cursor that you can move around with the thumbstick. Placing the cursor on your current location should keep your present location near the center of the screen as you zoom in and out. Make sure the position shown on the map agrees with your known location.

Marking Your Position as a Waypoint

You can now mark (or save) your present location as a waypoint. Press the BACK button to return to the main menu and use the thumbstick to scroll to the "Mark Waypoint" window, indicated with a red flag (fig. 33). Push the thumbstick, and you should see a screen similar to that in figure 34, whose name is displayed at the top of the screen. It is probably an automatically generated number as shown. To change it to the name you want, such as HOME, scroll up to the name with the thumbstick and push it to get an alphabetical keyboard. Scroll with the thumbstick to the letter "H," push the thumbstick, do the same for all the other letters, and finally scroll down to "Done" and push the thumbstick to display the new name, along with its coordinates and elevation. Scroll down to "Done" and push the thumbstick again to return to the main menu.

Figure 33. Garmin eTrex 20 main menu: "Mark Waypoint" selected

Figure 34. Garmin eTrex 20 Mark Waypoint screen

Traveling to a Waypoint

To recall your waypoint, start from the main menu and scroll to "Waypoint Manager" (fig. 35) with the thumbstick, push it, and all of your waypoints will be displayed (fig. 36). Scrolling to a particular waypoint shows its distance and direction (such as 0.31 mile SE), below the waypoint name. Once you've made your selection, pushing the thumbstick shows a new screen with the coordinates of the waypoint and the word "GO" should be highlighted at the bottom of the screen. Pushing the thumbstick displays a route line from your present position to the selected waypoint. Set the direction (such as SE) on your baseplate compass, and travel in that direction (as explained in appendix B). Once you are moving, select the "Compass" screen (fig. 37) from the main menu to display the distance and direction to your waypoint.

Figure 35. Garmin eTrex 20 main menu: "Waypoint Manager" selected

Figure 36. Garmin eTrex 20 Waypoint Manager screen showing list of waypoints

Figure 37. Garmin eTrex 20 Compass screen showing distance and direction to waypoint

Regardless of what operation you are doing at any time, you can always return to the main menu by pressing the BACK button repeatedly until the screen stops changing. The Back function stops at the main menu. (The MENU button on the left side of the unit allows you to restore the factory default settings or to perform some other functions unique to the particular screen you have selected.)

The **Magellan eXplorist 610** (fig. 15, page 37) is very different from the other two receivers in that it has a touch screen, allowing more flexibility in its operations. Much can be done with the touch-screen motions of tapping and swiping the screen with your fingertip. The operation of eXplorist models 510 and 710 are almost identical to those described here for model 610; the only difference between the 510, 610, and 710 is the types of preloaded maps. (The eXplorist GC, 110, and 310 have push-button controls and operate differently from the touch-screen units.) Upon turning it on, the Map screen is displayed. Without a position fix, it shows the last location the unit was tracking.

Four-Corner Menu

Tapping near the center of the screen reveals menus at all four corners (fig. 38). Tapping the upper left corner icon brings up the Dashboard screen, showing a variety of useful information. Tapping on the center icon at the bottom of this screen brings up a screen with nine icons (fig. 39). Tapping on the "Satellite" icon reveals the satellite status (fig. 40). The word "Tracking" along with a series of dashes in the accuracy box means the unit is searching for an adequate number of satellites. When TRACKING changes to FIXED, and the accuracy in feet or meters is displayed, the position has been found. As more satellites are found, FIXED may be replaced by GOOD or EXCELLENT as the accuracy number decreases.

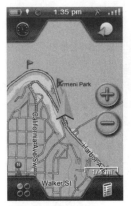

Figure 38. Magellan eXplorist 610 four-corner menu screen

Figure 39. Magellan eXplorist 610 dash-board selection screen

Figure 40. Magellan eXplorist 610 Satellite Status screen

If the accuracy shown is less than about 30 feet (10 meters), it is likely that you have a solid 3-D position. Larger numbers indicate a less-than-trustworthy 2-D position. To find out for sure, return to the Dashboard screen and tap on the "Data Only" icon, revealing much data. One item of interest is the elevation in feet or meters. If this is slowly varying, you have a 3-D position. If it is frozen (not changing), you have a question-able 2-D position. As you wait, the estimated accuracy should improve. Note that there is a primary and a secondary coordinate system, and the last numbers of these are also slowly changing.

Main Menu

Tapping the arrow in the lower left corner of the screen returns you to the Map screen, which shows your position on the map with a yellow arrow. Tapping the screen again reveals menus at all four corners. Notice the four little circles in the lower left corner. Tapping on this icon shows the main menu: a screen with nine icons, including "Waypoints," "Tracks," and "Routes," and a wrench and a screwdriver in the center of the band at the bottom of the screen (fig. 41). This is the Tools screen, and tapping on it brings up a new screen that includes "Settings." Tapping on "Settings" brings up another screen with several options, including "Units." And tapping on "Units" allows you to select feet or meters, kilometers or miles, and other options.

Figure 41. Magellan eXplorist 610 main menu

Coordinate Systems and Map Datum

Navigation is also under Settings (fig. 42), and tapping on it reveals primary and secondary coordinate systems (lat/long or UTM) and datums (fig. 43). Change from the default lat/long and WGS 84 to UTM and NAD 27 if you will be using it with USGS topo maps. If you are using the receiver with marine navigation charts showing only lat/long coordinates, use the default coordinate system.

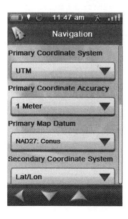

Figure 42. Magellan eXplorist 610 Navigation screen: UTM and NAD27 selected

Figure 43. Magellan eXplorist 610 Navigation screen: WGS 84 selected as secondary map datum

Saving Your Position as a Waypoint

If your receiver has a preloaded map, you should be able to find a Map screen that shows your position. You can zoom in and out to select whatever scale you want. Examples are shown in figures 44 and 45. To save (mark) your position as a waypoint, tap on the Map screen to get the four-corner menu, and tap on the four little circles to get the main menu. Tap on the "Waypoints" icon to get to the Waypoints screen (fig. 46), then tap on the "Options" icon in the lower right corner, which brings up the Options menu (fig. 47). Tap on "Add Waypoint," then on "Current Location." This brings up a listing of data for the waypoint, with the name of the last saved waypoint.

Tapping on the waypoint name brings up the first half of an alphabetical keyboard (fig. 48). The other half is accessed by tapping the black right-pointing arrow under the letter "k." From the second half of the alphabet, the first half can be accessed by tapping the black left-pointing arrow under the letter "v." You can switch between uppercase and lowercase letters by tapping on the upward arrow under the letter "i." You can rename the waypoint to whatever name you want, such as

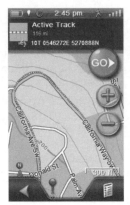

Figure 44. Magellan eXplorist 610 preloaded map: moderate zoom selected

Figure 45. Magellan eXplorist 610 preloaded map: much closer zoom selected

Figure 46. Magellan eXplorist 610 Waypoints screen

Figure 47. Magellan eXplorist 610 Waypoints Options menu

Figure 48. Magellan eXplorist 610, half of the alphabetical keyboard

HOME. When done, tap the check mark in the lower right corner. Then tap the "Options" icon and then "Save." Your waypoint is now saved with the name you chose.

Traveling to a Waypoint

To travel to any previously saved waypoint, go to the main menu, tap on "Waypoints," and scroll through your list of waypoints using the up and down arrows until you find the waypoint you want to travel to. Once you find it, tap on the orange circle with an arrow at the bottom of the screen (fig. 49). You may see a note saying "Cancel current route and start new one?" To go to your newly chosen waypoint, tap on Yes. Now go to the Dashboard screen and tap on "Data Only" (fig. 50). The list of data shows the compass bearing (labeled "Bearing") and the distance (labeled "Distance to Next"). You can set this bearing on your compass and travel toward your destination. Alternatively, use the built-in electronic compass, but it must be calibrated and checked before use. To calibrate the compass, return to the Tools screen, then Settings, and scroll to Calibrate Compass and follow the on-screen directions.

Figure 49. Magellan eXplorist 610 Waypoint Detail screen, showing data for selected waypoint

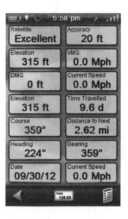

Figure 50. Magellan eXplorist 610 Data Only screen

GO FOR A WALK

Having saved a waypoint that identifies your home location, write down the coordinates and go for a walk in your neighborhood, where you know all the roads, streets, and directions. Keep the GPS receiver turned on the entire time. Watch the display as you walk to gain an appreciation of how the numbers change as you move. For example, if you live in an area with a grid of streets running north–south and east–west (see fig. 51), you might try walking directly east. While doing so, you should see the UTM easting number increasing while the northing number stays relatively unchanged. At the first corner turn right and start walking south. If you do, then the easting should stay relatively constant but the northing number will start to decrease. At any point you can switch to the Map screen and see your track displayed as a solid or dashed line.

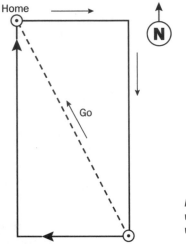

Figure 51. Go for a walk to gain familiarity with your GPS receiver.

At some point in your walk, stop and ask the receiver to tell you how to get home. As mentioned in the preceding section, select a Waypoint screen, and display a list of waypoints. Select the waypoint labeled HOME, and the receiver displays the distance and direction to your home. Check to make sure that this makes sense and agrees with your understanding of your neighborhood, how far you have traveled, and in which direction. Then walk back home, either by reversing your original route or by taking an entirely different route. When you reach home, one of the screen selections should show you how far it is to home. Don't be surprised if it says you have 30 feet (10 meters) left to go when you are actually at your doorstep. This is within the achievable degree of GPS accuracy, though you may often get a closer agreement.

It is important to note the difference between the terms *course, heading, bearing,* and *course deviation* as used by GPS manufacturers (see fig. 52). *Course* is the direction, in degrees, from your original starting point to your destination. *Heading* is the direction in which you are actually traveling at any point in time. *Bearing* is the correct direction you should be traveling in order to reach your destination at any point in your trip. If you are off course, *course deviation* is the distance by which you are off course.

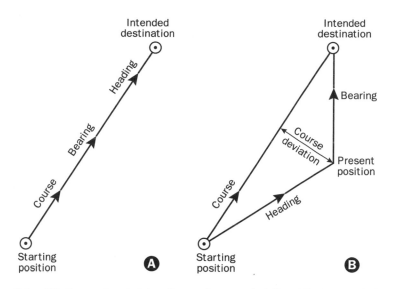

Figure 52. Course, bearing, heading, and course deviation; (A) at start of trip, course = bearing = heading; (B) after getting slightly off-course.

Once you get home, you should have a good appreciation of what your receiver can do. You should have seen how it acquired a position, displayed that position with a set of numbers, and allowed you to save that position as a waypoint. Then as you traveled, it should have responded to changes in your position. At some point you told it to GO to your previously saved position, and it showed you the distance and direction to get there. These are the primary functions of any GPS receiver. Once you understand and can do these tasks, all the other things that the receiver can do are merely refinements of these basic principles.

ADVANCED GPS FUNCTIONS

Eventually you will need to take the time to read the entire instruction manual and try out all the features of your receiver. But reading the manual will be a lot more meaningful and interesting for you if you first go through the familiarization process described above. When you sit down to read the instruction manual, be sure to have your receiver close at hand. Most of us learn best by actually doing, rather than by reading or listening, so try out each function as it is described.

Up to this point we have described the primary essential functions of GPS receivers: finding and displaying your position (orientation), and finding the distance and direction to any previously saved waypoint (navigation). Another important function is to define a waypoint without actually having been at that location. For example, you may be able to see the location of a certain place on a topo map, but you have never actually been there, so you have not yet saved a waypoint for that location. All but the simplest GPS receivers have the capability to do this. The exact method depends on your specific receiver, but in general the procedure is the same: get your receiver to display any previously saved waypoint. Select the name of the waypoint, which should bring up an alphabetical keyboard, change the waypoint name to your new destination, and select the UTM or lat/long coordinates, which should bring up a numeric keyboard, and you can replace the previous waypoint's coordinates with those for your new destination based on map data. After altering the waypoint with the name and coordinates of your new destination, save the new waypoint and navigate to it just as you would to any other waypoint.

Electronic Compasses

Without a built-in magnetic compass, the GPS receiver only displays your heading while you are moving. It records successive position changes and, from this, figures out the direction in which you are moving. With a built-in compass, the receiver can tell which way it is pointing, even when you are standing still, as long as it is properly calibrated. If you have a receiver with a compass, you can tell if it is calibrated by pointing it in a known direction and observing if the Compass screen agrees with the direction it is pointing. If it is not, then you need to calibrate it using a specific set of directions in your quick start guide.

Electronic compasses in GPS receivers frequently go out of calibration when the batteries are changed, when it is bumped or jarred, the receiver is not used for an extended period of time, and sometimes for no apparent reason. It is important to avoid using the electronic compass in any critical situation and to always carry a baseplate compass whose operation does not depend on battery power.

Bells and Whistles

Beyond the essential operations of orientation and navigation, a GPS receiver can perform a variety of other functions, "bells and whistles" that might nevertheless be helpful. Familiarize yourself with these operations by reading the instruction manual carefully. Some receivers have map functions and can accept detailed topo maps purchased separately on SD or micro-SD cards. Others can accept maps uploaded from a computer. (See chapter 6 for interfacing your GPS receiver with a computer.) If you wish to use your receiver in the wilderness, it is best to obtain 1:24,000-scale topo maps for your area of interest. These are available from the manufacturer of your GPS receiver or may be preloaded into the receiver.

Some GPS receivers, in addition to displaying a Compass screen, can show other data such as your speed, the distance to the next waypoint, the estimated time to travel to that waypoint, and the estimated time of arrival at that waypoint. Some receivers also have a "Trip Computer," with additional data, while others have a MOB (Man Overboard) function that allows for the rapid creation of a waypoint and quickly initiates a route to that waypoint.

Most receivers have the capability to create routes between a series of different waypoints: you navigate to the first waypoint, then to the next, and so on. Most receivers will create a "track" of closely spaced waypoints if you leave it turned on throughout your trip. Then, on returning to your starting point, you can switch to a "backtrack" mode, by which you retrace your steps.

Other functions available in some GPS units include geocaches, calculators, calendars, alarm clocks, stopwatches, rising and setting times of the sun and the moon, tidal data, and estimates of the best times to hunt and fish. Some receivers have built-in cameras or radio transceivers allowing the sharing of data with other receivers. We recommend a careful reading of your user's manual to become fully acquainted with all of the capabilities of your receiver.

TAKE A HIKE

Once you are comfortable with the basic operations of your new GPS receiver, bring it along on a familiar hike. At the trailhead or other starting point, turn it on and acquire a good 3-D position. Note the automatically assigned waypoint number (such as WP005), or rename it as you like (such as PKG LOT or CAR).

Enjoy your hike, occasionally looking at the receiver's screen to see how close its displayed position is to your actual position on the map. From time to time, ask it to GO back to your initial waypoint, and it should give you the distance and direction to your car. Ask it to GO to your intended destination, and it should tell you how far it is (as the crow flies) and in what direction. By switching to different navigation screens, it can also tell you your average speed, estimated time of arrival, and other potentially useful information. The best way to become an expert GPS user is to use it in familiar areas before you travel in unfamiliar territory.

GO ON A ROAD TRIP

Though this book is intended for wilderness GPS usage, it can be fun and instructive to use the receiver as a passenger while someone else is driving. Most receivers, even basic ones, contain preloaded base maps showing most major roads, so you can follow your progress and compare the receiver's displayed location and speed to the known location and the speedometer. You can also observe such trip parameters as distance to a waypoint, cross-track error, velocity made good, and others (as explained in the unit's instruction manual). Comparing the GPS unit's display with information that you know from another source will help you to learn all its important features as well as become more confident and competent in its use as you zip by bridges, rivers, and other recognizable features visible on the electronic map, all at much higher speeds than achieved while walking.

Chapter
4

Using GPS in the Wilderness

The most important rule for using the GPS unit in wilderness travel is to avoid becoming completely dependent on it. Use your map and compass as primary navigational tools and your GPS unit as a backup, or vice versa, or some combination of the two. In no case, however, should you ever completely depend on a GPS receiver.

There are many ways that you can use GPS for navigating in the wilderness. Remember that there are two main tasks that GPS can do for you: identifying your precise point position (orientation) and showing the way to your intended destination or objective (navigation). With these capabilities in mind, the following sections will identify a variety of different ways of using GPS to aid in your wilderness travels. As you learn to work with your GPS receiver, you may discover other ways to use it as well.

GPS AS A BACKUP NAVIGATIONAL TOOL

In wilderness travel we frequently use the GPS receiver as little as possible and primarily as a backup. This method is ideal for those who want to maximize their enjoyment of the wilderness: the forests, flowers, wildlife, and other aspects of the scenery, as well as the companionship and camaraderie of friends or other group members, or the pleasures of solitude, while getting back to nature and away from the complexities of civilization and technology. This method is also effective in maximizing the life of the receiver's batteries.

When using the unit as a backup, you are carrying a good quality paper topo map of the area as well as a conventional baseplate compass. Select and follow a route based on topographic and human features in order to simplify navigation and minimize physical difficulties. You may be following a route described in a guidebook or provided by a friend or fellow wilderness traveler. In any event, find the route on the topo map and study it to identify and deal with any potential route-finding difficulties. When you actually go on the trip, follow roads, trails, and topographic features such as ridges, gullies, streams, or passes to get to your destination. The GPS is not a part of your route plan, but you take your unit along anyway, as a backup navigational tool.

To use this method effectively, you need to turn the GPS unit on and save waypoints at the beginning of your trek and at critical locations along your route, such as trail junctions, ridge crests, stream crossings, and places where your route changes. The rest of the time the receiver can be turned off and safely stowed in your pack.

Example: An Off-Trail Scramble

Suppose you hike up a trail to a small lake, head cross-country up a hillside to the top of a ridge, and follow the ridge crest to the summit (see fig. 53). At the lake, you take a rest stop to have a snack. This is a good time to turn on the GPS receiver, find your position, and take and save a waypoint. Give it a name such as LAKE if you wish, or, since you might be in a hurry, merely let the receiver give it a sequential name such as WP004. If you do this, it is wise to make a pencil mark such as #4 at the lake on the map to remind you of the receiver-generated name of the waypoint. Turn off the receiver, place it back in your pack, and head up the hill.

Once you reach the ridge crest, you anticipate turning right and following the crest of the ridge up to the summit. Realizing that this precise spot will be important on your return, you might want to mark the spot by building an easily spotted rock cairn or by marking a tree with a streamer of toilet paper (which should be easily visible on the way down, but which will completely disintegrate after a few rainstorms). As a backup, you take the GPS receiver out of your pack, turn it on, and acquire and save another waypoint after confirming that it is a valid 3-D position. You could call it RIDGE or accept the receiver-generated name, such as WP005.

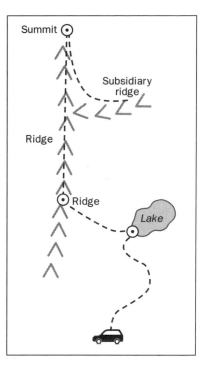

Figure 53. Example of using GPS as a backup navigational method

Climb the ridge crest, eventually reaching the summit where you sit down to enjoy the view and have your lunch. You might also turn on the GPS receiver and acquire and save another waypoint.

Getting Lost on the Descent

Eventually you decide to head back down, so you start descending along the ridge. But at some point, you realize that your surroundings look unfamiliar. You encounter an abrupt rock face just below that you know you did not ascend on the way up. You conclude that you must have somehow gotten off route. How do you get back on route? This might be difficult, since you do not really know where you are. But with the GPS unit as a backup, you can turn it on, let it acquire a 3-D position, and find out exactly where you are.

If your receiver does not display topo maps, you can read the UTM easting and northing coordinates on the display and find their intersection on the paper topo map you are carrying. If your GPS unit displays topo maps, it should show your exact position without using UTM coordinates or your paper map. Either way, your receiver can display the distance and direction (bearing) to the previously taken waypoint on the ridge (WP005). You can then start hiking following that bearing and using your baseplate compass.

If at any time you find it impossible or inconvenient to travel in a straight-line path toward that point, you can deviate from that bearing and travel on the most convenient route in the general direction of WP005. After you pass the troublesome point, turn on your receiver, let it acquire a position, ask it to GO to the desired point, and then travel by compass bearing to the new bearing displayed on the GPS receiver. Even if your receiver has a built-in electronic compass, it would be wise to travel using your baseplate compass anyway, since GPS compasses often go out of calibration and give incorrect readings. By now you are using the GPS receiver frequently to get to your intended destination, so you decide to leave it on all the way down, rather than turning it off and on at frequent intervals. Since you are carrying spare batteries, you are not afraid of your batteries dying.

Eventually you reach the point where you originally encountered the ridge crest. You tear down the cairn or remove the streamer of toilet paper and head downhill to the lake. You find the trail and hike back to the car. You never planned on using the GPS to navigate toward the destination or back but used it as a backup when you got off route.

GPS AS THE PRIMARY NAVIGATIONAL METHOD

Using GPS as a primary navigation tool is a method similar in some ways to that used by our friend who crossed Greenland. When using this method, you know the exact location of your destination. In the Greenland crossing example, Chuck actually went to the end destination and took and saved (or marked) a number of waypoints using the GPS receiver. That is one way to get a waypoint into a GPS receiver, but it is not the only way. You can also find the coordinates of your intended destination on a topo map and enter them into your GPS unit, as explained in chapter 3. At any point in your trek you can ask your receiver to GO to that waypoint. You can find the distance and bearing to the new destination on one of the navigation screens and set your compass to match that bearing. And you can turn off the receiver to conserve battery power and travel by compass bearing using your baseplate compass. (See appendix B for specific directions for following a compass bearing.)

Example: Ice Fishing Trip

Suppose you are trying to get to a specific point on the surface of a frozen lake to do some ice fishing (see fig. 54). Your friend Ron found a good spot and placed a fishing shelter there. He saved a waypoint for this spot on his GPS receiver, and he tells you the coordinates and invites you to go to this favorite fishing spot and use his shelter while he is on vacation in Florida. The UTM coordinates he gives you are as follows:

15T 3 32 941 mE
52 29 896 mN 1532 feet

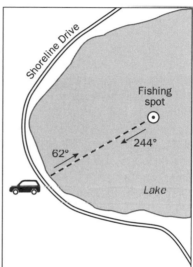

Figure 54. Example of using GPS as the primary navigational method

Before leaving on the trip, you turn on your own GPS receiver and let it acquire a location. You save (or mark) this waypoint, and the receiver gives it the name WP087 and your current UTM coordinates. (See appendix A for a complete explanation of the UTM system.) You then edit the waypoint, giving it the new name FISH SPOT and changing the UTM coordinates to match the numbers that Ron gave you (it is not necessary to enter the 1532-foot elevation). Next, take out your paper USGS topo map of the area and locate the fishing spot on the map at the intersection of the easting (mE) and northing (mN) coordinates. On the map you also find a place to park since it is early in the winter and the ice is not thick enough to support the weight of your car. Enter the parking location into your receiver, giving it the name CAR.

GPS will be your primary navigational method since conventional map and compass techniques are not accurate enough. If you are off course by only 5 degrees in 1 km (a little more than half a mile), your position error could be about 100 yards—the length of a football field. You need far better accuracy than that, since Ron's fishing shelter is a commercially available type used by many other anglers. You don't want to be caught trying to get into the wrong shelter and risk an unpleasant confrontation. You will bring your paper map and your baseplate compass as backup navigational tools, but the GPS unit is your primary method.

On the day you go fishing, you drive to Shoreline Drive and park your car. Take out your GPS unit and let it acquire a good 3-D position and label it CAR. To ensure that it is a good position, compare its UTM coordinates with those you previously measured on your paper map. They agree with your known position, so click into your cross-country skis and ask the receiver to GO to the previously entered waypoint called FISH SPOT. It tells you that this waypoint is at a bearing of 62 degrees and is 1.1 km away. Set your baseplate compass to 62 degrees and turn the GPS receiver off to conserve battery power. Then ski along the frozen lake surface, following the compass bearing. After about twenty minutes, take out your GPS receiver, let it acquire a good 3-D position, and ask it to GO to the same waypoint. This time it tells you that the waypoint is 0.2 km away, at a bearing of 66 degrees. Reset your compass to 66 degrees, but this time, since you are quite close to your target, you leave the receiver on as you approach the shelter. Soon you see two identical-looking shelters rather close together, one a little north of the other. Once you are close to the northern of the two shelters, the receiver tells you that you are 15 meters (about 50 feet) away from your destination, which is a bit too far off given modern GPS accuracy capabilities. So you go to the southern shelter, at which the receiver says you are 5 meters (about 15 feet) away, and well within the margin of error for your receiver. Sure enough, you see Ron's initials on the shelter. Within minutes of dropping your line, you get a bite.

Oops!

After a few hours of fishing, you have caught your daily limit and are ready to go home. You look out and see that it has begun to snow, heavily enough that you can no longer see the lakeshore. But you are confident that you can get back without difficulty, using the GPS. Turn the receiver on and let it acquire a position, then tell it to GO to the waypoint named CAR. It says to go at a bearing of 244 degrees for 1.1 km, so you set your compass for a bearing of 244 degrees and turn the receiver off and set it down. While packing up your gear for the return trip, you accidentally kick the GPS receiver into the fishing hole! The receiver quickly sinks into the frigid depths. You will have to make it back to shore without using the GPS receiver.

Recovery

Thankfully, your compass is set for a bearing of 244 degrees, which should get you back to your car as long as you can travel at exactly that bearing for a little more than half a mile (fig. 55). But if you are off-route by even a little bit, you could miss your target and reach Shoreline Drive at a location other than where your car is parked. You might wonder whether you should travel to the left or to the right, since you would not know the direction of your error. This situation can often be avoided by using a technique known as "aiming off." In this case, set your compass 10 degrees less than the required bearing (234 degrees rather than the correct 244 degrees), so when you reach Shoreline Drive you know that you are to the left of your car and you can then turn right. Ski while following the bearing of 234 degrees, turn right when you reach the road, and find your car a few minutes later. Sorry that you lost your GPS receiver, you are nevertheless grateful for your stringer of fresh fish. And you were looking for an excuse to upgrade to a newer unit anyway.

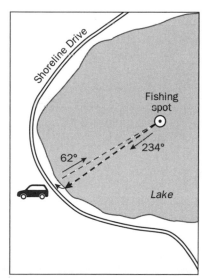

Figure 55. "Aiming off" to ensure that you turn in the correct direction as you near your destination

CREATING AND FOLLOWING COMPLEX ROUTES

The previous example assumed that you could follow a straight-line path from your origin to your destination. Many times this is not possible due to the presence of obstructions or inconveniences such as cliffs, mountains, rivers, or lakes. In other situations, straight-line travel might be theoretically possible but requires excessive up-and-down travel. In cases like these, you might choose a more topographically sensible path instead, in which you contour around obstructions in order to avoid them, or take a path following trails and ridges to facilitate easier travel. For these kinds of situations, it makes sense to create a *route* consisting of a series of previously defined waypoints. Most GPS receivers have the capability of doing this, and most receivers can store multiple routes, which can be activated at any time. You can easily create a route by stringing together a number of waypoints, where the direction from one waypoint to another is approximately a straight line. When traveling on such a route, the navigational information shown on the screen of the receiver will be more sensible and meaningful than if your entire route consists only of your origin and your destination.

Example: A Complex Route

Suppose you are planning on doing a scenic loop trip in the mountains, as shown in figure 56. You start at the trailhead at point A, hike up the

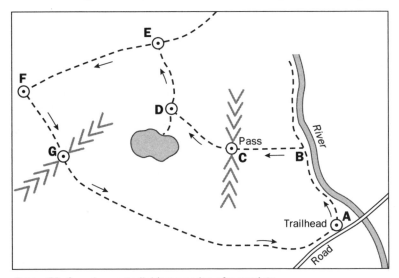

Figure 56. Complex route linking a series of waypoints

trail following the river to point B, where you head cross-country to the pass at point C. You go down from the pass to pick up a different trail at point D and head up that trail to the junction with another trail at point E. From there you hike to the sharp bend at point F, then up to another pass at point G, and finally close the loop on the trail back to point A. Each segment of the route is relatively straight, so the navigational parameters displayed on your GPS receiver will be more meaningful.

Since you have never traveled this route with a GPS receiver, you will have to find the UTM coordinates for all these points on a topo map. Do this at home, prior to the trip. These coordinates are estimated to the nearest 100 meters either by "eyeballing" to find the location between printed kilometer lines, or by using the meters scale at the bottom of the map. If your GPS receiver has a preloaded or downloaded topo map of the area, you can select the location of interest by using cursors with left-right-up-down buttons or with a thumbstick. If your receiver has a touch screen, you can create a waypoint by tapping on the location to create and save a waypoint. Do this for every waypoint on your route. Give the route a special name such as LOOP TRIP, and save it by choosing a SAVE or DONE command.

BACKTRACK

Most GPS receivers have a variety of track features, such as active track, track history, route line, and point destination line. These allow you to see your progress on a map. In addition, if you are doing an out-and-back trip, you can select a backtrack route that shows the distance and bearing from wherever you are back to the previous waypoint in your route. This allows you to return to your starting point over the same route that you followed on the way in. Study the features in your receiver's instruction manual to learn about how to implement them; each receiver type has its unique methods and terminology.

POWER ON OR OFF MOST OF TIME?

For most wilderness travel, we recommend leaving the GPS unit turned off most of the time, and only turning it on from time to time to obtain and save waypoints or to determine the required direction of travel. This saves battery power. However, it is helpful in some situations to leave the receiver on for extended periods of time, such as navigating a technical rock or glacier climb with route-finding challenges. This practice will obviously use up battery power much more quickly than sporadic GPS usage, so be sure to bring one or more sets of spare batteries. Leaving the receiver on all the time allows it to record your precise track, rather than just straight-line segments from one recorded waypoint to another.

Another situation in which you might want to leave your receiver on continually is if it is getting late and you are in a hurry to get back before dark. Under these conditions, you will not wish to stop, turn the receiver on, and wait for position fixes. Leaving the receiver on allows you to look at the receiver any time you need to, saving valuable time.

It is usually inconvenient to hold the receiver in your hand all the time since you might prefer to use that hand to hold an ice ax or a ski pole, to put in climbing protection, to scramble over rocks or fallen logs, or to paddle. For this reason, it is a good idea to find a way to attach your receiver or its case to your pack strap or watercraft or some other convenient place where you can see its screen and manipulate its controls. Then you can concentrate on the details of the activity, while still seeing the details of your route on the screen of the receiver. A word of caution: When using this method, you might be tempted to use the GPS unit so much that you miss the scenery, wildlife, flowers, or even a trail junction. Remember that the GPS unit is a means to an end, not an end in itself.

Using GPS on the Water

Having a handheld GPS receiver on board your kayak, canoe, sailboat, or rowboat greatly simplifies navigation on the water, but you still need to know basic marine navigation and carry a magnetic compass and a set of navigational charts or topo maps covering the areas in which you will be traveling.

Navigation on the water differs from land navigation in one crucial way: marine navigation usually involves charts labeled with latitude and longitude coordinates, whereas land navigation involves topo maps labeled with the UTM grid as well as latitude and longitude. Beyond this difference, GPS usage on the water is very similar to that on land. If you intend to use the GPS in any aquatic application, we recommend that you read chapter 4 carefully as well since some material in that chapter is applicable to both situations but is not repeated here.

GPS RESOURCES FOR MARINE USE

Our discussion of using GPS receivers on the water is restricted to human-powered craft without electrical generators or other forms of electrical power other than low-voltage cells. This restricts us to using the same sort of handheld GPS receivers also used for hiking and other land-based activities, as described in chapter 2. The basic receivers can be used in much the same way on water as on land, with the possible exception of using the latitude-longitude grid rather than UTM, in order to correlate with locations shown on marine charts. If you need both hands for paddling, it is helpful to get a receiver that can be worn on the wrist, or one that is waterproof and can float if dropped into the water. A few of these are identified in chapter 2.

Intermediate and advanced receivers are capable of displaying detailed topographic maps for land navigation, and most of them also have provisions for the use and display of marine navigation charts. Both Magellan and DeLorme receivers make use of Navionics Gold or HotMaps Premium charts for most areas of the world. These contain all the data that are found on conventional marine navigation charts, plus updated information from cartographic surveys, notices to mariners, and the Navionics community of user-generated content via internet downloads. The charts include tides, currents, wrecks, port plans, marsh areas, marine services, and other useful data. A purchase of either of these products includes unlimited updates for a full year. Garmin receivers make use of a similar set of charts called BlueChart g2. If you are a serious saltwater paddler, we suggest that you invest in an intermediate- or advanced-level receiver and also a set of these charts for the areas in which you intend to travel. Once you have downloaded the chart set, print out whatever portions you need for travel in your area of interest. Plan on carrying the paper copy in a waterproof case, along with a clear ruler and a baseplate compass as a backup to GPS navigational techniques.

Freshwater GPS users who will be paddling on rivers, streams, and lakes will be better off using standard USGS topo maps, which show many of these water features, as well as dams, waterfalls, rapids, and marshes, and the surrounding topography of the land. They can do most navigation by using the UTM grid and a basic-level receiver, or by using an intermediate- or advanced-level receiver with map viewing capability, just as with land navigation.

If your route closely follows a saltwater shoreline, you might have your choice of using either USGS topo maps or marine navigation charts, or both. The USGS topo maps usually show more detail of land features such as inlets, harbors, and topographic features, and show coordinates in UTM. The marine charts show coordinates in latitude/longitude, and give more information of interest to mariners, such as rocks, shoals, shipping lanes, and other hazards. It might be advisable to carry both: USGS topo maps for more detail of small areas, and marine charts for larger areas where less detail is needed. If you are switching between topo maps and marine charts, it is helpful to get a receiver such as a DeLorme Earthmate or a Magellan eXplorist that can display UTM and lat/long, one being the primary and the other a secondary coordinate system.

Some receivers have profile settings that allow you to customize your receiver for different types of activities, such as hiking, geocaching, or marine activities, such as paddling. If your receiver has such a function, it is best to set it to marine, which customizes the GPS receiver's display to show various values in marine units, such as nautical miles and knots rather than statute miles and miles per hour.

TRIP PLANNING

Begin your trip planning at home, using resources such as your home computer and paper or digital marine charts or topo maps. You can plan your trip as a series of straight-line segments in open water, paralleling a shoreline, or following a river or stream. You can select either a series of waypoints and connect them as a route, as described in chapter 4, or trace out the entire route on your home computer and upload that route to your receiver (see chapter 6). In this case the GPS receiver will be your primary navigational tool, and conventional techniques will be used as a backup as needed. Alternatively, you can simply hope for good visibility all the way and never go far from shore, so that you can do all your navigation using visual piloting methods. In the latter case, a GPS receiver will be a backup navigational tool, available for your use in the event of heavy fog or getting off course due to unexpectedly strong tides, winds, or currents. You can save waypoints at noteworthy spots such as where you change direction, and plan on not using the GPS receiver unless you run into trouble.

GPS AS THE PRIMARY NAVIGATIONAL METHOD

Since the GPS is so much easier to use than conventional marine navigational methods, it makes sense to use it as your primary method. But be fully knowledgeable of conventional techniques in the event that your GPS receiver fails you, and carry paper charts and a marine or baseplate compass, or preferably both. Your kayak may be equipped with a marine compass mounted on it, reading magnetic bearings and headings. In addition, it is helpful to also carry a baseplate compass so that you can measure bearings to visible objects on land, such as hills, mountains, docks, or buildings, to help you determine your location. If you will be using a marine compass whose display is magnetic bearings, then you should also set your GPS north reference to magnetic.

Plan your trip ahead of time by reading up on the route, studying navigation charts, plotting out your path on a paper chart, and creating and saving your intended route. When you reach your launch point, take out your receiver to acquire a waypoint and ensure that it matches the waypoint you previously loaded into the receiver as your starting point. Actuate the route you stored on the receiver at home and note the bearing toward the next waypoint. Then push off and start paddling. Follow the bearing shown on the GPS receiver and read the heading to ensure that these two directions are the same. If not, turn your vessel to make the heading match the bearing. Once you reach the desired waypoint, you may need to turn to head toward the next waypoint. The receiver keeps telling you the correct bearing to your intended destination, as well as your actual heading, and you take whatever action you need to take to stay on course.

If you get off course for any reason, the receiver will display a new bearing, and you can turn your craft until your heading once again matches the required bearing. You will probably want to keep the receiver turned on all the time and maintain operation on the same screen until you reach a convenient point to beach your vessel and take a break.

At your first stop, you might look at your receiver and observe navigational statistics such as average speed, velocity made good, cross-track error, and estimated time of arrival. You might also decide to change the displayed data if the data you saw on the last leg of the trip did not include some parameter that you considered important, such as your present speed.

You can continue this procedure for your entire trip. If your batteries become exhausted or if you accidentally drop the receiver into the water and lose it, you will need to resort to conventional marine navigation methods involving the paper chart and the magnetic compass.

Example: Kayaking to an Island

Suppose you are planning a kayak trip from shore to an island to visit a friend (see fig. 57). Though it is not a long trip, there is a complication due to the presence of a small island that blocks a direct route. In order to minimize the amount of open-water travel, your route plan is to paddle from shore at point A to near the island at point B, then detour about 90 degrees past the east end of the island to point C, back to the original heading until past the island at point D, back to your original bearing at point E, and then follow a straight-line route to your friend's waterfront home on the next island at point F. This is easy to do using GPS methods.

You can find all six waypoints on a navigation chart at home before the trip. If you have a marine chart and a basic-level GPS receiver such as those listed in table 1 in chapter 2, you can find the coordinates of each point on the chart using the coordinates given at a corner of the chart. Then measure the distances from that corner to each point of interest and find the number of degrees, minutes, and seconds (or degrees, minutes, and decimal minutes) to add to the corner coordinates, using the scales printed along the edges of the chart. (See appendix A for an example of this process.)

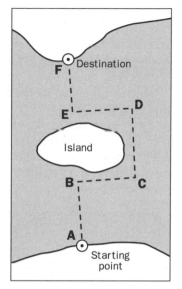

If you have an intermediate- or advanced-level GPS receiver as listed in table 2 or 3 in chapter 2, you can define the six waypoints using the Map screen of the receiver and call them waypoints A through F. If you have marine navigation charts on your home computer, you can

Figure 57. Kayak route around island

identify all six waypoints and download them to your GPS receiver, assuming that it has the required connectivity features (see chapter 6).

Once the waypoints are defined, you can create a route on the receiver, usually by selecting a "Route" icon and entering the six waypoints. After saving the route, you should be able to follow that route all the way from the mainland to your friend's island home. Your receiver will display the magnetic bearing for each leg of the journey, and you can keep your vessel pointed in that direction, as indicated on your marine compass, until you reach each waypoint. Wind, currents, waves, and swells might push you off course from time to time, but the GPS receiver will always tell you the new bearing to follow to get you on track to your destination.

When you are ready to return to the mainland, you can either select the backtrack feature on your GPS receiver or define a new route from point F to A. On each leg of the trip, your receiver will display the required magnetic compass bearing for that portion of the route. Now suppose that while paddling from point F to point E, the batteries in your GPS receiver give out, and you have no spares since you did not anticipate that the trip would take as long as it did. How will you get to points E, D, C, B, and A? By using conventional navigational techniques.

One such method is shown in figure 58. You might be able to use this method if the island is small and if there is some identifiable point, such as a radio tower, a church steeple, or a lighthouse that you can see from both sides of the island. Take out your baseplate compass and take a bearing on the object, then paddle around the island, paralleling the shore, until you are on the other side of the island. With your baseplate compass take a *back bearing* on the object. (A back bearing is just the reverse direction to the original bearing, and you can find its value by adding or subtracting 180 degrees. For example, the back bearing of 240 degrees is 60 degrees.) If the back bearing does not match the opposite of the original bearing, continue paddling until it does. Then you can return to your original bearing to get home.

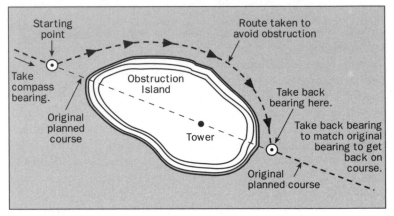

Figure 58. Navigating around an obstruction when you can see an identifiable landmark

If the island is large, or if there is no identifiable object on which to take a bearing and a back bearing, you might have to resort to a different method, as shown in figure 59. Keep paddling until you near the island at point E, turn 90 degrees to your left and keep going until you clear the island at point D. During this leg you must carefully keep track of the time it takes to go from E to D, since this will be about the same amount of time that you will need to travel to get from point C to B. Instead of tracking time, you could count paddle strokes. After you reach point C, you can travel the same amount of time or strokes until you reach point B. After you reach point B, turn another 90 degrees to get back to your original bearing.

As you paddle home, reflect on the difficulty of trying to stay on the original bearing line while navigating around an obstruction and you

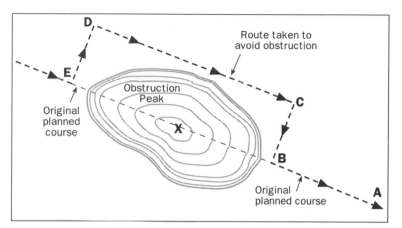

Figure 59. Navigating around an obstruction when you cannot see a well-defined point from both sides of the obstruction

will appreciate the GPS more than ever. You promise yourself that you will never again go on a kayak trip without a spare set of batteries.

CONVENTIONAL NAVIGATION AS THE PRIMARY METHOD

There may be times when you wish to navigate primarily by using old-fashioned chart and compass techniques, either to keep those skills current in your brain, or just for the mental challenge involved. In this case, plot out the course and measure compass bearings at home before the trip, then try to follow your planned trip on the water. If you get off course, you will need to figure out exactly where you are by using buoys, lighthouses, landmarks, and other conventional techniques, then plot out the new bearing to your intended destination and set a course for that point, navigating by chart and compass. If these methods do not work, or if you grow impatient with them, you can always resort to the use of the GPS, assuming that you have been taking and saving waypoints at important places along the way.

Example: Kayaking to the Eagle's Nest

Suppose you are planning to take a kayak trip to observe an eagle's nest some distance north along the coast (see fig. 60). The shoreline is somewhat irregular, with points, bays, and coves, and you will need to travel between several islands and the shore. The entire route will be near the shore, which is dotted with convenient lighthouses, radio towers, church steeples, and other landmarks. There is no need for GPS on this trip since it will be a simple job of piloting your craft from one visible landmark to another. You decide to take your GPS receiver anyway, as an added precaution. You don't bother to try to identify the coordinates of each point along the way, since you don't need them.

You put in at point A and take and save (or mark) a waypoint. You paddle to point B, where you need to turn to traverse the channel between the island and the shore. You stop and save a waypoint. You do the same at points C, D, E, and F, not planning to use them but simply as a precaution and because you want to upload the route to your computer once you get back home. After rounding point F, you see the eagle's nest at point G. You beach your kayak and unload your camera, tripod, and binoculars.

After observing for several hours, you will see a thick fog

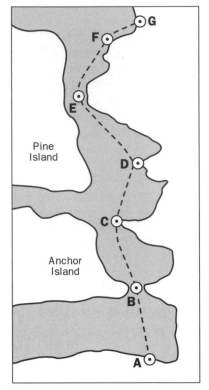

Figure 60. Example of using GPS as a backup navigational method

coming in and quickly enveloping the area beyond you. There will be no visible landmarks on the way home. Fortunately, you have taken and saved all the waypoints that you need. You define a route from point G to A, passing through all the other five waypoints along the way. You keep your eyes open along the way in case you suddenly come close to another craft, and you listen carefully for foghorns that might alert you to the presence of a large vessel approaching. You can tell from looking at your marine chart of the area that there are no commercial shipping lanes along this route, but there still could be vessels in the area that could present a significant hazard. As you approach point B, you notice that the fog is burning off, and you get back to your starting point without incident.

Interfacing a GPS Receiver with a Home Computer

The GPS device on its own is a great tool, but when you connect it to your home computer a whole new world of functionality emerges. If home computer functionality is important to you, include it on your list of needs when choosing a GPS receiver. Usually it is a bit more expensive, but the connectivity feature is well worth it if you use it.

INTRODUCTION TO COMPUTER INTERFACING

Be sure that your GPS receiver is compatible with the Mac operating system if you are a Mac user. (Almost all devices by default work with the Windows operating system if they have computer connectivity at all.)

Internet and Physical Connections

If you seek home computer compatibility, internet access is a must, especially if you wish to download plug-ins, additional software, and updates. Fast connections are obviously better, particularly for high memory applications such as detailed topographic maps.

A physical connection between your GPS receiver and computer is necessary for the two to communicate. Often this is through a USB cable, likely provided if the GPS receiver has home computer capability.

Sometimes the USB port is obvious; sometimes it is not and may be hidden in the battery compartment. Refer to the quick start guide for its location. A small minority of advanced GPS receivers have wireless Bluetooth connectivity with a home computer, but the two devices will need to be paired in order for them to communicate with each other. Follow the receiver's instructions on how to make such a connection.

Once you have connected your GPS unit to your home computer, see if your computer recognizes your device, either through the "Finder" (Mac) or "My Computer/Devices" (PC). Be sure that your GPS device is turned on when you do this. It may be necessary to go to the receiver's Settings screen and select "Connect to Computer."

If you are sure that your GPS device has computer compatibility, yet it does not show up as a device, try restarting the computer while the device is attached and powered on. Patience is occasionally required here.

Once the GPS device is recognized it is likely that you will need to download additional software from a CD supplied with the receiver or from the internet in order to use the GPS receiver with your computer. Following the on-screen directions, install any software that you need in order for your GPS unit to communicate with your computer. A computer restart may be necessary. Also be sure to register your unit using on-screen directions.

Software Upgrade

Once the GPS device is recognized by your home computer, it is possible that the device will need a software upgrade. If so, follow the on-screen directions. If there are no on-screen directions, you may have to download the user's manual (if a printed one was not included in the box) and follow those instructions.

Removable Memory

Many GPS receivers have an SD or micro-SD slot (sometimes hidden behind the batteries) to accept portable memory. This is used to transfer maps and as expandable memory for screenshots and photographs. Removable memory can also be used to transfer waypoints and routes that you have selected or programmed from your GPS receiver to your home computer. If your home computer has the same type of slot for the memory card as your GPS device, you can simply insert it into the slot. If your computer does not have such a slot, you can purchase a separate card reader. Many printers also have SD or micro-SD card slots for digital cameras that you can use as an interface with your computer. Micro-SD cards can be used in regular SD card slots by using a small, inexpensive micro-SD to SD adapter.

Trip Planning and Analysis

Once you have established communication between your GPS device and your home computer, you have the ability to program a route and its waypoints on your home computer in the comfort of your home, and then to transfer it to the GPS receiver, either directly though the cable or by saving your route to the SD card and inserting the card into your GPS device. The websites for the receivers (www.garmin.com, www.magellangps.com, www.delorme.com, etc.) usually have a "My Device" or similar option to allow you to do this.

Using the GPS unit and home computer interface also allows you to analyze a trip once completed. On your trip you may have collected data via your GPS device, such as your starting point, waypoints, tracks, and other GPS data. Once you return home, your device can be connected to your home computer to analyze the data, or to share it with friends. You can often display your rate of elevation gain, speed of travel, distance traveled, and other information. With the more advanced receivers or programs, the level at which you wish to explore the data is seemingly unlimited.

BRAND-SPECIFIC SOFTWARE

DeLorme units use Topo North America software. Garmin uses Base-Camp, and Magellan uses VantagePoint. All of these are included in the purchase price, though for Garmin units, the actual 1:24,000-scale topo maps are available at added cost. Some GPS device instruction manuals are sketchy with regard to how to use these software packages. If you have difficulties, go to the manufacturer's website to find customer support, technical support, or help. URLs are usually given in the quick start guide or owner's manual.

BRAND-SPECIFIC INSTRUCTIONS

All of the above-mentioned software programs are powerful tools, capable of performing a wide variety of useful tasks. The rest of this chapter will explain three specific things that all of these programs can do: define a waypoint or a route on a map, export waypoints or routes from the computer to the GPS device, and import data from the GPS device to the computer. Once you have learned how to do these tasks, we urge you to learn all the other features of your software program as well. Explore what happens when additional features are selected, and don't be afraid to read the owner's manuals or "Help" functions that come with these programs. These instructions apply to the latest software versions that we know of at the time of this writing. Future revisions of these programs may require somewhat different actions, but will probably not differ too much from those described herein. As with many software packages, there are often multiple ways of accomplishing many software tasks. In order to keep this section as simple as possible, we have identified just one method for doing each of the tasks. You may discover alternate ways of doing the same task.

Garmin

Download BaseCamp software from www.garmin.com.

Familiarize yourself with BaseCamp by watching the short video presentations that explain what BaseCamp does and how to use it.

To create a waypoint on your computer: The homepage (fig. 61) is a base map with only major highways and roads. If you have added area topo maps to your Garmin GPS device, these will also be visible if your device is connected. First, click on the map selection tab (A) to get a dropdown menu, and select the topo map you want displayed (Topo US 1:24,000 Northwest in fig. 61). (The default map is the "Global Map," a "basemap" that only shows main roads.) A blue triangle (B) is visible in the upper left corner of the map. Hover over it and it turns into directional arrows and a zoom bar. Pan and zoom to show the area where you want to locate a waypoint. Click on Tools (C), then Waypoint, and the cursor turns into a small square. Position it at the waypoint location and click. An automatically generated name will appear, which you can highlight and rename to whatever you want. Repeat to place and name other waypoints. When done, click on Tools, then Pan to remove the small square.

To transfer waypoints and the route from your computer to your GPS device: With your GPS device connected via the USB cable, click on Edit (D), then Send To. Click on the name of your GPS device (e.g., eTrex 20). You can send waypoints and routes or create lists of waypoints and routes, and select which list you wish to send.

To transfer waypoints and the route from your GPS device to your computer: With your GPS device connected, click on Edit (D), then Send To, and highlight the desired list on your computer. You can send waypoints, routes, and tracks. To change measurement units, coordinate system, map datum, etc., click on Utilities (E). To change the Send To or Receive From device, click on Device (F).

Magellan

Download VantagePoint software from www.magellangps.com.

Familiarize yourself with the toolbar and icons: The homepage of VantagePoint is a map (see fig. 62 below). Hover over the blue direction

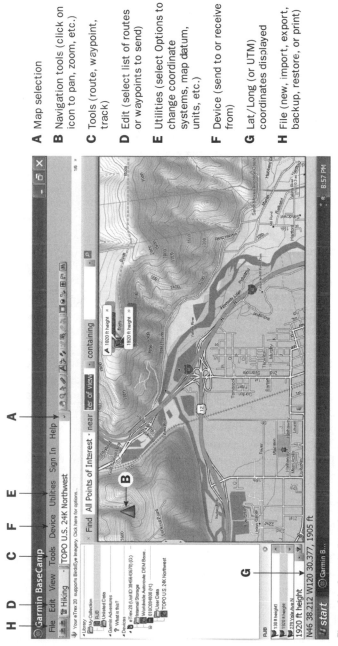

A Map selection

B Navigation tools (click on icon to pan, zoom, etc.)

C Tools (route, waypoint, track)

D Edit (select list of routes or waypoints to send)

E Utilities (select Options to change coordinate systems, map datum, units, etc.)

F Device (send to or receive from)

G Lat/Long (or UTM) coordinates displayed

H File (new, import, export, backup, restore, or print)

Figure 61. Garmin BaseCamp homepage

and zoom buttons (A) in the upper right corner of the VantagePoint map. Use these to pan and zoom to display the position you want. On the toolbar (B), hover over each of the symbols to see their purposes. To return to the homepage map, use the "Select" arrow (C) near the left end of the toolbar.

Click on the red "Waypoint Pin" (D) on the toolbar. A dropdown menu gives you three choices: Waypoint, Geocache, or Contact. Click on Waypoint.

Your cursor turns into a small square. Use the mouse to position this symbol at the exact spot you want, then click and follow the on-screen directions to name and save the waypoint.

Your cursor remains a small square so you can define additional waypoints in the same way. When you are done generating waypoints, click on the "Select" arrow (C) on the toolbar to return to the Home screen.

To transfer waypoints and the route from your computer to your GPS device: With the VantagePoint homepage displayed and your GPS device turned on, connect your GPS device to the computer. Soon the device screen changes to one displaying "Connect to PC." Select this and the device screen says "Connected to PC."

The computer screen should display the same dropdown menu as it does whenever additional hardware is detected, giving you a choice of options. Click on Take No Action. On the toolbar's Sync section (E), hover over the second icon (F) and it should display "Transfer from PC to My GPS." Click on this and follow the on-screen directions to transfer your data, and click OK. The screen should say "Data transfer has been finished successfully." When you are done transferring waypoints, click on the "Select" arrow (C) to return to the Home screen. Disconnect the USB cable and check the Waypoints screen on your GPS device to make sure the waypoints are there.

To transfer waypoints from your GPS device to your computer: While VantagePoint is running on your computer, connect your GPS device and turn it on. Select "Connect to PC" when it is displayed. When the external device dropdown menu appears, select "Take No Action." Hover over the third icon in the Sync section (G). It should display "Transfer from My GPS to PC." Click on this, and follow the on-screen directions to transfer your data, and click on OK. Click on the "Select" arrow on the toolbar to return to the Home screen. After you disconnect your GPS device, the waypoints should remain displayed on your computer.

Other features: The "Preferences" icon (H) allows you to change the coordinate system, map datum, measurement units, and north

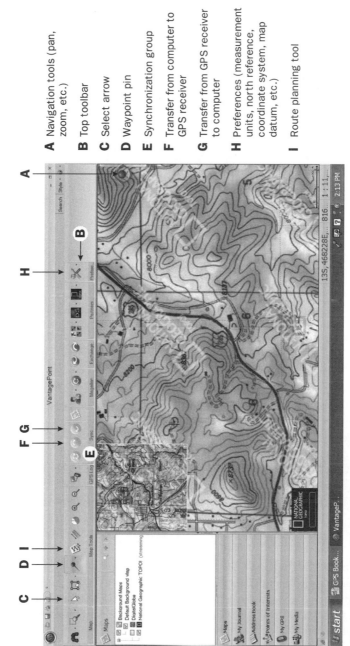

A Navigation tools (pan, zoom, etc.)

B Top toolbar

C Select arrow

D Waypoint pin

E Synchronization group

F Transfer from computer to GPS receiver

G Transfer from GPS receiver to computer

H Preferences (measurement units, north reference, coordinate system, map datum, etc.)

I Route planning tool

Figure 62. Magellan VantagePoint home screen

reference. The Route Planning Tool (I) can be used to create new routes or modify existing routes.

DeLorme

Insert the Topo North America CD into your computer's drive to load the software. The home screen first asks if you want to Create a new project (such as a planned wilderness trip) or Open a recent project. Whichever option you select, a detailed topo map (see fig. 63) appears with navigation tools (A) in the upper right-hand corner, allowing you to pan and zoom to anywhere in North America. Pan to display the area of your planned outing, and zoom in to get the best scale.

Familiarize yourself with the toolbars and icons: The upper toolbar contains an icon labeled "Options" (B). Clicking allows you to change the measurement units to statute or nautical miles, or to kilometers; you can select the map coordinate system (lat/long, UTM, or others) and the appropriate map datum to agree with that shown on your paper map. Most USGS topo maps printed in 1988 and later use the NAD 27 datum, indicated by "Horizontal Datum" in the lower left corner of USGS maps.

The top toolbar also contains a "Help" icon (C). Clicking on it, then on "Help Topics" displays a dropdown menu, directing you to instructions on how to create a route (go to Getting Started, then to How do I? then to How do I create a route?). Another option is a tutorial explaining the use of the "Sync" (synchronization) function, used to transfer data between your computer and GPS device. Access this by scrolling to Using Earthmate PN-Series GPS Devices, then to Syncing Maps and Data, then to Tutorial: Sync Data with a PN-Series GPS. You should read these two topics carefully if you wish to create waypoints and routes on your computer and transfer data between your computer and GPS device. Be sure to explore other useful help topics, such as viewing and printing maps and transferring them to your Earthmate GPS device.

To create waypoints and routes on your home computer: Open a new project, and place your cursor on your point of interest (such as the intended starting point of your next wilderness outing) and observe the numerical display along the right side of the screen (D). The point's latitude/longitude or UTM coordinates (whichever you have selected) will be shown, and you can copy these down and manually enter them into your GPS device, as explained in chapter 3. Alternatively, you can automatically load this data into your GPS unit, as explained below. Start by right-clicking on the starting point, selecting "Create Route," and then "Set as Start." You can add stopping points (E) along the way

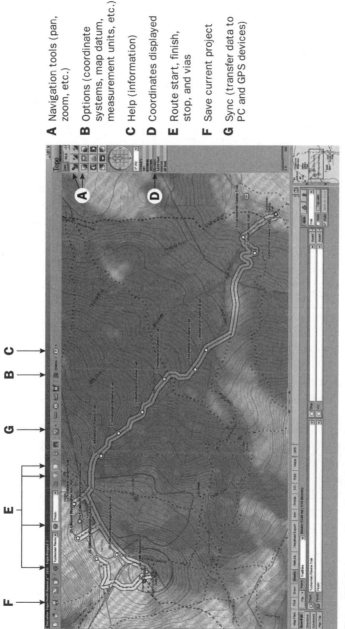

A Navigation tools (pan, zoom, etc.)

B Options (coordinate systems, map datum, measurement units, etc.)

C Help (information)

D Coordinates displayed

E Route start, finish, stop, and vias

F Save current project

G Sync (transfer data to PC and GPS devices)

Figure 63. DeLorme Topo North America home screen

such as lunch or campsites and finally a "Finish" waypoint. Save the route using the "Save" icon (F) on the upper toolbar.

To transfer waypoint(s) and the route from your computer to your GPS device: With Topo North America running, connect the GPS unit to your computer using the USB cable provided with the device. Turn it on and select the "Settings" icon, and scroll to Connect to Computer. Open the SD card and the internal drive as directed by the menu, and select "Use GPS."

On the computer, open the desired project and click on the green "Sync" icon (G). The computer will go through a short sequence of operations such as connecting, analyzing, and waiting for the SD card to be prepared. Eventually a two-sided pane will appear, showing the status of the PC and GPS data. The left side shows Topo North America (computer) data, and will say "Not all files on GPS." If you click on "Project Contents" at the bottom of this pane, you will see the name of the route you have previously defined. If the box to its left is blank, be sure to click on this box to place a check mark in it. The right side of the pane gives the status of the Earthmate PN-60 GPS receiver, indicating whether or not all its files are in Topo USA on the computer.

Now click "Sync" again, and you will see the computer going through a series of operations to synchronize the data. When finished, it will display Sync Complete. Click the "Close" box in the pane, and the computer will indicate that the PN-series device is updating. You can then disconnect the GPS device, and the waypoints and route will now be on the GPS unit as well as on the computer. You can now select the route and follow it as the GPS unit directs you from one waypoint to another.

To transfer waypoints, routes, and tracks from your GPS device to your home computer: Connect your GPS device to your computer and establish communication as explained above. Open Topo North America and select Create a new project, then click Sync. The two-sided pane will open, showing Not all GPS files are on Topo North America. Click on "GPS Contents" at the bottom of the GPS side, and observe the GPS data to be synced. Ensure that there is a check mark in the box(es) next to the data you want to transfer. Click on "Sync," and after a short time you will see a green check mark indicating Sync Complete. Click on "Close," and observe that the Earthmate device is updating. Disconnect the GPS device, and ensure that all the desired waypoint, track, or route data is now on your computer. The data should also still be on your GPS device.

National Geographic's Mapping Software

Until recently, National Geographic produced sets of seamless 1:24,000-scale USGS topographic maps on CDs for all of the United States called TOPO!. They could be purchased for approximately a hundred dollars per state. You can use these in a variety of ways to augment your GPS device.

Though National Geographic has discontinued this software, many people have purchased and still use this product, and so we will describe it here. (Copies of the TOPO! software are still available on some websites.)

A typical National Geographic TOPO! Map screen is shown in figure 64. Once you load the software, check the appropriate website for any updates and install them if necessary.

Familiarize yourself with the toolbar and its tabs and icons: Hovering over each icon explains its functions. Clicking on each tab reveals dropdown menus for available actions. A few specific actions can be done as follows:

To change the coordinate system or map datum: To be consistent with those of your paper map or chart, click on Preferences (A) on the toolbar and select the coordinate system and map datum.

To create waypoints and routes on your computer: One way to use the TOPO! software is to zoom in on your particular area of interest, click on Tool (B) on the toolbar, then Waypoint. The cursor turns into a small square, which you can locate wherever you want on the map. Click at that point to observe the latitude and longitude or UTM coordinates in the lower right corner of the screen (C), and manually enter these coordinates into your GPS device. This makes it unnecessary to "eyeball" or measure coordinates on the paper map. You can also go to Tool (B), then Routes on the toolbar and draw an actual route from one point to another on the screen of the computer. The route shows up on the map as a solid red line. At the bottom of the screen you will find the distance and an elevation profile indicating the amount of elevation gain and loss on the route.

To transfer waypoints and the route from your computer to your GPS device: Transferring waypoints and routes from the computer to the GPS device will do away with the need to enter UTM or latitude/longitude coordinates manually. Connect your GPS device to your computer, select Handhelds (D) from the toolbar, and establish communication between your computer and your GPS device. Once this is done, you can use the dropdown menu for Handhelds to select Export

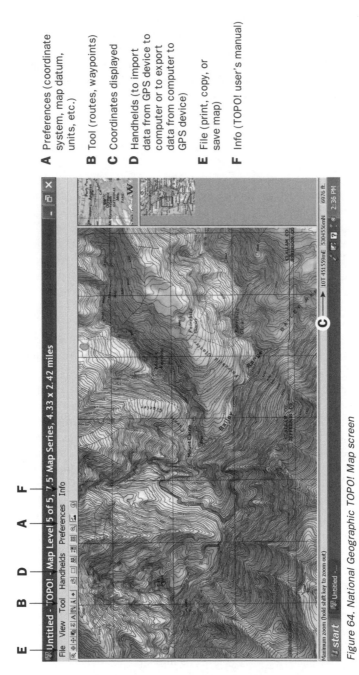

A Preferences (coordinate system, map datum, units, etc.)

B Tool (routes, waypoints)

C Coordinates displayed

D Handhelds (to import data from GPS device to computer or to export data from computer to GPS device)

E File (print, copy, or save map)

F Info (TOPO! user's manual)

Figure 64. National Geographic TOPO! Map screen

to GPS. Disconnect the receiver and check your receiver's waypoints or routes list to ensure that the transferred information is indeed there.

To transfer waypoints and the route from your GPS device to your computer: While on your wilderness excursion, you can save additional waypoints. If you leave the receiver on all the time, you can record your actual track on your GPS device. After you get home, connect your GPS device to your computer, click on Handhelds (D), establish communication with your computer, and select Import from GPS to import your waypoints or the entire track from your GPS device to your computer. You can print this out or send your track along with a digital map to a friend or associate. The File tab (E) on the toolbar allows you to select a New map, Save As whatever you want to call it, and to Print, Copy, and Export.

We have merely scratched the surface of the capabilities and features of TOPO!. If you have this software, be sure to click on Info (F), and Help Using Topo!, which downloads the TOPO! user's manual. If you don't want to read it all, then at least read the chapters entitled "For People Who Don't Read Manuals," and "Using TOPO! With a GPS Receiver."

Since discontinuing their TOPO! product, National Geographic has teamed up with AllTrails to produce the Ultimate Outdoor MAP KIT, an online mapping subscription-based tool that costs about 40 dollars per year and allows users to view and print satellite photos and various types of topographic maps for any area within the United States. It allows users to connect their Windows or Mac computers to their Android or iOS smartphones. However, it does not allow users to transfer waypoints, routes, or tracks between a dedicated GPS device and their home computer. The tool's most useful feature is to allow users to print portions of USGS and other topographic maps to take with them on wilderness adventures.

Cautions for Using a Computer to Obtain and Map Waypoints

While a computer is very handy for obtaining and mapping waypoints without the need to use UTM or lat/long, remember that you will not bring your home computer with you on your wilderness trips. There is always the possibility that somewhere along the way you may find it necessary to define a waypoint for a place you have not saved and will have to create one, or you might have to locate a position on a paper map or chart to identify your present position. For this reason, you should still learn how to use UTM to find a precise location on a paper topo map and how to use lat/long to find a position on a marine chart.

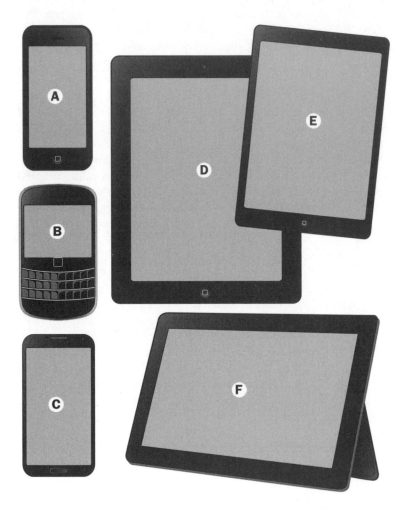

Figure 65. Typical smart devices: (A) iPhone, (B) Blackberry Bold, (C)Samsung Galaxy S4, (D) iPad, (E) iPad mini, and (F) Windows Tablet

Using the GPS with a Smart Device

DEFINING SMART OR MOBILE DEVICES

"Smart" devices are simply small, portable mini-computers. Examples of these include the Apple iPhone, Samsung Galaxy, Blackberry Bold, Apple iPad, and Windows Tablet (fig. 65). These are battery-powered devices that can receive signals from three sources: the cellular network, a Wi-Fi network, and GPS satellites. The ranges of these signals are as little as a few miles for cellular phone signals and several hundred feet for Wi-Fi signals. GPS signals, on the other hand, are available almost anywhere on Earth. Figure 66 shows the relative ranges of the three types of signals in relation to the user. This last point is critical because in wilderness travel you are often traveling outside of cellular range, and certainly well outside of Wi-Fi range. In the context of this book, mobile or smart devices include smartphones, tablets, PDAs, and other devices equipped with a GPS antenna and receiver and the corresponding software (apps).

We've focused much of this chapter on the mobile capability of the Apple iPhone and the iOS (Apple's mobile operating system), as these comprise approximately half of the smart devices used today. However, the following techniques, apps, and accessories, with modification, will most likely apply to many other devices and operating systems such as Google Android, Nokia Symbian, Samsung Beta, Microsoft Windows

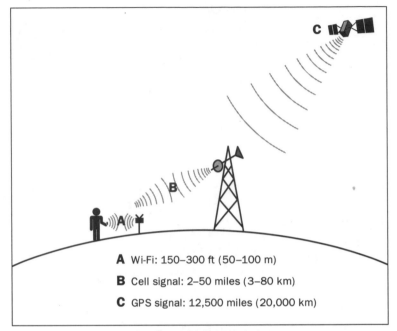

A Wi-Fi: 150–300 ft (50–100 m)

B Cell signal: 2–50 miles (3–80 km)

C GPS signal: 12,500 miles (20,000 km)

Figure 66. Comparative signal ranges of smart devices

Phone, and Blackberry, as long as they have a dedicated GPS receiver antenna built in.

THE GPS SIGNAL, WI-FI, AND THE CELLULAR NETWORK

Most smartphones and other similar devices have GPS capability and can display your position in lat/long coordinates and also your position on a digital map (see fig. 67). If topographic maps are desired for wilderness travel, these very critical maps are not transmitted to your device through the GPS satellite signal. The maps are best downloaded through a Wi-Fi connection, if one is available; if not, then through the much slower cellular network. If you have not downloaded the maps for the area in which you will be traveling, and you are out of Wi-Fi and cell tower range, your smartphone/mobile device may be able to display your position via the GPS signal, but only as a dot on a gray grid or a blank screen (see fig. 68). One trick around this is to "cache" a map of the area by panning and zooming into an area that you will be traveling to beforehand, while still in range of cell phone towers or a Wi-Fi network.

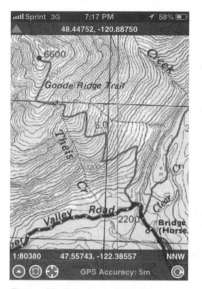

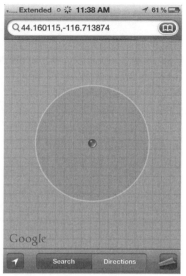

Figure 67. Topo map displayed
on screen of an iPhone: latitude/
longitude coordinates shown

Figure 68. Position from a GPS
signal when out of cell range

If you have not downloaded or cached a map of the area and get a dot on a gray grid, you may still be able to find your location by getting the device to display the latitude/longitude or UTM coordinates even if the map is not displayed. This data may even be embedded into a picture that you take. Locate the position data and find your position on the paper map that you should be carrying anyway. But remember number 4 of our quick start guide in the introduction to this book: You must always examine the coordinates carefully and make sure that they make sense to you, and that they are not merely the last known coordinates (a common default condition of smartphones as well as dedicated GPS receivers when the device cannot obtain a current satellite position fix), which could be miles away from your current position.

A simple test of this concept of GPS is to go on a hike on a familiar trail or on a ski tour that you know to be outside of cell phone range, but one in which you have not previously visited with your smart device, nor previously zoomed in on. Turn on your smart device, start up a GPS app, and see what happens. Is your location displayed in a gray field of little squares? Or is this position the device's last known position, such as your living room? Or is it a new position that agrees with your known location as shown on your paper map? If it is indeed a new position that makes sense to you, then you may be able to associate the latitude and longitude (or preferably UTM coordinates) to your paper map, but that may be all the GPS functionality that you get. Alternatively, your smart device may simply tell you that you are outside of the cellular network or that it cannot connect to the internet (fig. 69), politely telling you that it is only receiving half of the data: position only, without map data. Without a paper map, the coordinate is most likely useless for navigation.

THERE'S AN APP FOR THAT!

Many of today's higher-end smart mobile devices have a built-in GPS antenna and associated circuitry to process the signals. This allows them to receive GPS radio signals, which can be interpreted to indicate point position. To find out if yours has a dedicated GPS receiver, install one of the many free or inexpensive GPS apps, such as Where Am I At?, AllTrails, Green Trails Maps, Ski Tracks, AllTrails, or Google Maps. Some apps allow the display of your position coordinates in your choice of lat/long or UTM. Then go into your smart device's settings (be sure that the

Figure 69. Out-of-cellular-range message displayed on iPhone screen

Figure 70. Location Services means this smart device has a built-in GPS capability.

GPS is enabled), sometimes described as Location Services (see fig. 70) and turn off your Wi-Fi and cellular network access. This leaves only the GPS radio waves receivable. Start your GPS app and see what happens. Does it indicate a strong GPS signal? Does it give a location that makes sense to you? Does is give a location at all? If so, make note of it or take a screenshot. (On the iPhone, screenshots are taken by simultaneously pressing the HOME and SLEEP buttons.)

Now it's time for a short walk, drive, or bike ride to a familiar location. Leave the Wi-Fi and cellular network access off while doing so, to simulate wilderness conditions where you will have to do without them.

Once you are some distance from where you first obtained a GPS signal, fire up the GPS app and observe the GPS coordinates once again. Compare the new coordinates to the saved screenshot. Are they different? Do the new coordinates make sense? Oftentimes a GPS device, even a smart device, will display the last known position if a current position cannot be calculated. This is a critical concept and is why it is so important to double check the position that the device indicates against what makes sense. Bad information is worse than no information at all. If the new position agrees with your current position, then you have data that you can work with. Experiment with free apps and read reviews of apps that cost money to see if a particular app is worth the money for your particular needs.

In our quick start guide in the introduction, number 5 is to leave your trip itinerary with a responsible person. There are apps for that too! One in particular is Bugle (see fig. 71). Once the app is activated, if the user does not inactivate the failsafe messaging system upon returning from the adventure (or blind date, Craigslist meeting, or

Figure 71. Let others know your itinerary with an app such as Bugle.

other potentially risky endeavor), Bugle automatically transmits a message to selected contacts with instructions as to your trip details, route, and where to search for you if you do not report in as planned.

Another smart device accessory is an external communication antenna (and app) that allows the wilderness user to broadcast messages to the Iridium communication satellites, which provide 100 percent worldwide coverage. DeLorme inReach is a good example. When paired with a smart device (or DeLorme PN-60w GPS receiver), it allows you to communicate via SMS (short message service) with people back home, automatically transmit and update your track, update social media, and, most importantly, send a message out to request rescue. The inReach unit costs about $250 and the required subscription service will run you an extra $200 per year, depending on options. This may sound expensive to the wilderness traveler who only ventures out a few times a year, but it may be invaluable for those out every weekend, traveling alone, or on an adventure where electronic communication is necessary but otherwise impossible.

DIGITAL MAPS

The key to successful navigation with a smart device is downloading the map or maps of the area to which you will be traveling well before your journey begins. There are several apps you can purchase that allow you to download 1:24,000-scale topo maps. Be sure to do this with a strong Wi-Fi signal, as attempting to download detailed maps while driving to remote trailheads can be frustrating to say the least. Downloading the map may be as simple as zooming in as close as possible to your entire wilderness route. Your smart device may be smart enough to cache the map data and display it later once it is outside of the cellular network. Of course, you must test this first in a known location outside of cellular range to determine the capabilities of your particular smart device and to ensure that the scale and detail of the maps is of value to your adventure.

PRECAUTIONS WHEN USING SMART DEVICES FOR WILDERNESS NAVIGATION

A smart device is an excellent SMS device, a quality phone, an OK camera, a fairly good web surfer, a good portable media player, an OK SMTP (email simple mail transmit protocol) device, a flashlight, and, under perfect conditions (within range of cell towers, Wi-Fi, and GPS signals), a reliable GPS device. But there is one major, deal-breaker of a drawback.

Battery Life

Smart device users often complain about the limited battery life of their devices in metropolitan areas, where there is easy access to wall or car chargers. Just wait until you enable location services and/or GPS apps on your wilderness adventure! Powering up a GPS receiver on a mobile device has a tendency to suck your battery dry within a few hours! This all-in-one device, with only limited battery power remaining, gives users only fleeting access to GPS, Wi-Fi, cell phone, photography, and SMS.

There are, however, a few tips for extending your smart device's battery life while the GPS antenna is powered up. The first is to turn off power-hungry apps. (Ironically, powering up the GPS antenna for use with GPS apps is a highly battery-draining action!) With an iPhone, double-click the HOME button and hold down any of the icons in the dock. Minus signs will appear above all open apps (see fig. 72). Tap the minus signs to close all the other apps. This will help conserve battery life. When you are done navigating, you should close out the GPS app as well, unless you want your device to provide a track of your adventure.

To further save battery power on the iPhone, tap Settings, then Notifications, and turn off all apps that are in your notification center. This will prevent the device from waking up when that particular app is activated by an incoming message, a social media update, stock report, or news update, if you are in range.

Another useful trick is to turn down the brightness of the display and to decrease the amount of time that the auto-lock feature allows before automatically powering down the display. The display consumes much energy, and even a slight dimming will correlate to increased battery life. (That said, on a bright day above tree line, the dimmed display is harder to read.) Experiment with different settings for screen brightness to see just how bright the screen really needs to be in order to be usefully visible outdoors.

Figure 72. Circled minus signs at the bottom of the screen allow you to close apps to save power.

If you do not need to record every step of your track, the best way to conserve power is to turn off your device completely. To turn off an iPhone completely, press and hold the SLEEP button for about three seconds until "Slide Power to Off" appears and slide to "off." (To wake the iPhone, press and hold the SLEEP button until the Apple logo appears.)

One of the authors doing research for the text you are reading attempted this technique, accidently pressing the SLEEP button instead of holding it down until the slider appeared and later discovered that when he thought the device was off it was actually in the sleep mode! As the sun dropped close to the horizon, the magic hour revealed itself and a continuingly beautiful lighting condition was beginning to present itself. The author produced his iPhone only to discover that he only had 5 percent power remaining. The phone had been consuming battery power that whole time in his pocket! As his only device capable of taking photographs was rapidly becoming useless, he instructed the other author to "Take a lot of pictures" with his "real" digital camera since his phone/camera/GPS receiver/flashlight/etc. was all but useless when its battery life dropped into the single digits. This is an example of what can happen when you put all your eggs into one basket, and then trip.

It is good battery-saving practice to shut off your smart device completely, much like in occasional GPS use described earlier, and only turn it on at key landmarks, attain a good 3-D position fix that makes sense, save the waypoint, and turn off the device. In this way the smart device is only used in emergency route-finding situations. As a minimum a good 3-D position fix must be taken at the trailhead (see our quick start guide, number 3). You do not want to be in a situation in which you discover yourself lost and turn on the device to somehow bail yourself out without a reliable waypoint to GO to!

Supplemental Power Sources

Supplemental power sources exist for smart devices in the backcountry, but you must consider the practicality of these accessories. External battery packs, integrated smart device protectors/supplemental battery accessories such as Mophie, and solar chargers can be carried to extend the battery life of your smart device, but how many external battery packs are you going to carry for the duration of your next trip, for the amount of time that you plan on using your receiver? How will you attach and arrange a solar panel array on your backpack to charge your smart device? Will it be effective as you hike in the forest? You can also purchase camp stoves that have the ability to charge your phone while cooking. But ask yourself, how much fuel do you plan on burning to charge your smart device?

LIMITATIONS OF GPS USAGE WITH SMART DEVICES

The fundamental message here is that if you are accustomed to using your smart device in the city, within cell tower range, and with ample access to power (such as from your wall socket, car, or computer), you cannot be afforded such luxuries in the wilderness. A different mindset is required in the backcountry. While in the wilderness, it is essential to turn off any app that you do not absolutely need. Otherwise, you may turn on your smart device to take a beautiful photo of your wilderness experience only to discover that your smart device is automatically powering down because it has so little battery power remaining.

Smart devices are amazing, compact, do-it-all devices that may be fun to take into the field, but due to limited battery life and other factors described above, they do not yet replace dedicated GPS receivers, and certainly are no replacement for traditional skills in paper map and compass techniques for wilderness navigation.

Coping with the Limitations of GPS Receivers

A variety of conditions and situations can occur that might prevent the GPS from giving you the information you need for navigation in the wilderness. We have previously mentioned some of these: deep canyons or heavy forest cover that prevent acquisition of enough satellite signals to obtain a position; outside temperatures below the minimum required for the receiver's LCD display; large inaccuracies caused by multipath signals due to reflections of satellite signals; exceeding battery life; losing or damaging your receiver; and electronic failure. These conditions are generally rare, and in many cases preventable. Still, such conditions can and do occur. Although it is impossible to counteract all possible unfortunate conditions, with a little forethought and planning it should be possible to get to your objective and back home safely even without a functioning GPS receiver.

EXTRA RECEIVER(S) TO DEAL WITH POSSIBLE GPS FAILURES

One obvious preventive measure, particularly when traveling in a group, is to carry two or more receivers. These devices are becoming more popular and more affordable, and when planning a wilderness trip it is often easy to find at least one other person in the party who also has a GPS receiver. The random failure of one receiver could be overcome, but it might not help if the loss of usage is due to a problem affecting both receivers, such as extreme cold, deep canyons, or excessive forest cover. If your navigation plan involves using a GPS receiver as your primary navigational tool, seriously consider carrying at least a second receiver on your trip.

COPING WITH GPS INACCURACIES

Modern GPS receivers are capable of very accurate operation, but only under certain conditions, including a clear view of most of the sky and after obtaining a dependable 3-D position fix. In addition, certain rare conditions, such as signal reflections off cars or cliffs, can cause outlier position fixes, often hundreds of feet or meters away from true positions. For these reasons, you should not mindlessly use or save any position until you have first verified its accuracy and reasonableness. (See number 4 in our quick start guide in the introduction.)

A good check on the accuracy of your indicated position is to find your UTM position (if your receiver does not display topo maps) and find that position on your paper map or your position on the preloaded or downloaded topo map, if you have that capability. An outlier will easily show up if you take the time to do this check. In addition, the receiver itself probably has an accuracy estimate in one of its data fields, usually on the Satellite Status screen. Look at this field to get a rough idea of the accuracy of the displayed position, though these are just rough estimates based on satellite geometry and signal strength. Before saving any truly important waypoint, ask yourself if the displayed position makes sense to you.

COLD-TEMPERATURE OPERATION

Every GPS receiver has a lower temperature operating limit, below which it will not display any data, due to inherent characteristics of its display. Various receivers have different temperature requirements, but generally this lower limit is somewhere around 0 degrees F (-18 degrees C). You can usually find this information in the specifications section of the owner's manual. If you contemplate using the receiver in such conditions, you should test the receiver's cold-temperature operation at or near your home in cold conditions (such as in your freezer) before you trust it to operate in a cold climate. If you need it to operate at a temperature lower than its lower limit, you might resort to carrying it close to your body, in a pocket or other location under several layers of clothing. Most receivers are not permanently damaged due to exposure to cold temperatures, and many still operate and can track your position under cold conditions but simply cannot display your position.

MAXIMIZING BATTERY LIFE

Many GPS users complain that their receivers use batteries at a faster rate than advertised. There are a few things that you can do in order to increase battery life.

In many cases you can use longer-lasting lithium batteries rather than standard alkaline batteries. Lithium batteries cost more but may save you money in the long run since they last longer. Furthermore, they work more reliably at cold temperatures and weigh less.

If you operate your GPS receiver at a moderate temperature, its batteries will last longer. You should keep the receiver and spare batteries out of direct sunlight, and inside your jacket on cold days.

Some receivers allow you to reduce trackpoint resolution to one per 1000 feet or about a quarter-mile rather than the more frequent position tracking that is the default trackpoint setting. Be sure to check your owner's manual to see if this is an option for your receiver, which will allow you to increase battery life.

Turn off your receiver when navigation is easy or straightforward, such as while walking along a good, well-maintained trail, as well as when in heavy forest cover or in a canyon where the unit will waste power trying to search for insufficient signals. Disable the WAAS

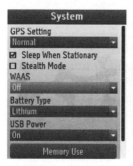

Figure 73. Disable and enable WAAS on the DeLorme Earthmate PN-60w receiver.

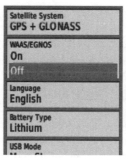

Figure 74. Disable and enable WAAS on the Garmin eTrex 20 receiver.

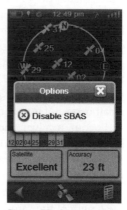

Figure 75. Disable and enable WAAS (SBAS) on the Magellan eXplorist 610 receiver.

function if you do not have a clear view of the horizon, since it takes extra battery power for the receiver to keep searching for a satellite that it cannot find. Some receivers have WAAS permanently enabled so this may not be an option. See figure 73 for an example of DeLorme's Earth-mate: Go to Settings, System, press ENTER, and choose WAAS on or off. Garmin's eTrex (fig. 74) is similar: from the main menu, go to Setup, System, and observe the Satellite System screen. You can then turn WAAS/EGNOS on or off. For the Magellan eXplorist, from the main menu go to Tools, Satellite, and Options. You should see a screen similar to that of figure 75, allowing you to enable or disable SBAS (Space-Based Augmentation System: the combination of WAAS and EGNOS).

Additional battery-saving techniques include reducing backlight brightness and the "timer off" period for the display screen's light dimmer. Most receivers allow you to set the brightness and timer off time to lesser values than the default conditions. Also, disable power drainers such as the compass, barometer, and altimeter if they are not being used.

CONVENTIONAL MAP AND COMPASS NAVIGATION

Another essential method of coping with GPS problems is your ability to fall back on conventional map and compass navigation techniques. We have warned against becoming totally dependent on your GPS receiver. Always carry a compass and a paper topographic map of the area in which you are traveling, even if the receiver has an electronic compass and a digital map of the area. If you do have a paper map with you, then you should be able to locate your starting point on the map and follow along on the map as you travel. Whenever you reach identifiable points along the way, such as trail junctions, stream crossings, ridges, gullies, passes, summits, lakes, and other landscape features, you can find them on the map. If you keep track of your position this way, you will always know your general position on the map, at least to within a small degree of uncertainty.

If your receiver should fail for any reason, you can locate your approximate position on the map by finding the last position (such as a stream crossing or trail junction) at which you were truly certain of your position. If you combine this knowledge with the approximate speed and direction that you were traveling since that time, along with the length of time since you did know your exact position, you should be able to estimate your present position at least roughly. This method of orientation is greatly facilitated if you know and can recognize topographic features such as gullies, ridges, saddles, and summits on the map (see appendix A). If you know your exact position, we say that you know your *point position*. From this, you can usually work out the direction and route to your objective or back home.

Line Position

Another way to identify your position without using the GPS is to identify some trustworthy *line* at or near your position, such as a road, trail, stream, ridge, lakeshore, or other feature. This is called *line position* and is generally not sufficient to ascertain your point position. However, if you can also find one other piece of trustworthy information, you might be able to pinpoint your location along that line, and thereby arrive at your point position. For example, if you are in the mountains, you might know your elevation if you are wearing an altimeter watch. The place where that identifiable line (such as a trail or a stream) crosses a contour line at your elevation will most likely indicate your point position.

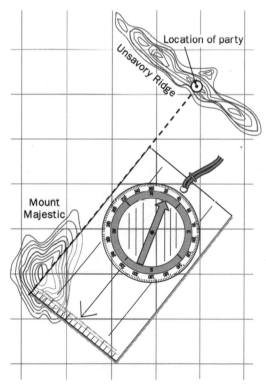

*Figure 76.
Orientation with
line position known
(magnetic needle
omitted for clarity)*

Another way of getting point position from line position is to take a compass bearing on a visible object, such as a mountain peak, and plot this bearing until it crosses your known line position, as shown in figure 76. This intersection indicates your point position. (See appendix B for instructions on measuring and plotting compass bearings on a map.)

Area Position

If you do not even know line position, you have what is called *area position*. Area position is the least desirable form of orientation. For example, you may know that you are somewhere west of Lake X or in a basin south of Peak Y. In this case, you might be able to take compass bearings on two identifiable objects and plot them to find your point position, as shown in figure 77. Or, if you know your elevation from

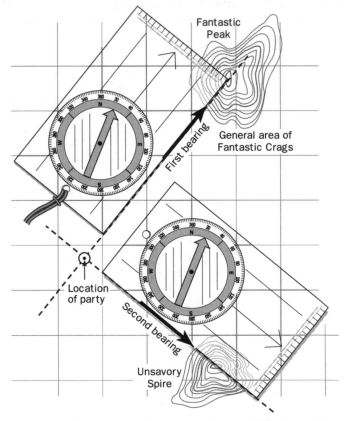

Figure 77. Orientation with area position known (magnetic needle omitted for clarity)

an altimeter, you might be able to take a bearing on one identifiable landmark and plot it on the map. The point where it crosses a contour line at your known elevation is your likely point position.

Recognizing Topographic Features

Another limitation of GPS receivers is their inability to indicate topographically reasonable routes. For example, asking it to GO to some waypoint from your present position gives you a straight-line path, possibly going up and over a mountain, across a lake, or off a cliff. It is often not practical to follow such a straight-line path, due to inconveniences or obstructions along the way. This is another reason that it is essential to carry a topographic map of the area, so that you can find a practical route from your present position to your objective, even if your GPS receiver is operating properly. By carefully studying the topo map, you can generally find an alternate route to your objective, to minimize the effort and inconvenience of getting there. (See appendix A for the interpretation of topographical features.)

If you are carrying a topo map of the area, you can also use the map, perhaps aided by your compass, in the event that your GPS receiver fails. If you know where on the map you are, and the location of your objective, it is usually possible to find a reasonable route between the two positions by studying the topography alone. If topography is not enough, then you can always measure the compass bearing from your location to your objective, and travel at that bearing, guided by your compass. (See appendix B for an explanation of these principles.)

Chapter
9

Lost

The primary focus of this book is to give you the necessary skills and knowledge to avoid getting lost in the first place. Later in this chapter we will give you some suggestions concerning what to do if you ever *do* get lost. But if you have carefully read and absorbed the preceding eight chapters, have adequately practiced using the GPS receiver as well as map reading and compass use, and carry a GPS receiver, a compass, and a topographic map of the area, you should always know where you are and will not get lost.

HOW TO AVOID GETTING LOST
Before the Trip

Most wilderness orientation, navigation, and routefinding is done by simply looking at your surroundings and comparing them to the map, or by finding your GPS position and verifying that it is correct. This process is often aided by making some navigational preparations before the trip, like identifying *handrails*, *baselines*, and possible routefinding problems.

A *handrail* is a linear feature on the map that you can follow, or it may be a feature that parallels the direction in which you are heading. The handrail should be within frequent sight of the route so it can serve as an aid in navigation. Features that you can use from time to time as handrails during a trip include roads, trails, powerlines, railroad tracks, fences, borders of fields and meadows, valleys, streams, cliff bands, ridges, lakeshores, and the edges of marshes.

A *baseline* (sometimes called a *catch line*) is a long, unmistakable line that always lies in the same direction from you, no matter where you are during the trip. It does not have to be something you can see during the trip. You just have to know that it is there, in a consistent direction from you. A baseline can be a road, an obvious trail, the shore of a large lake, a river, a powerline, or any other feature that is at least as long as your trip area. If the shore of a large distant lake always lies west of the area you will be in, you can be sure that heading west at any time will eventually get you to this identifiable landmark. Heading toward this baseline may not be the fastest way to travel back home from your destination, but it may save you from being truly lost.

Before the trip, it is wise to prepare a *route plan* and to trace out the entire trip on a topographic map. Identify handrails, baselines, and other features that you will be following on the way to your objective. Part of this plan is to recognize potential routefinding problems. For example, if the route traverses a large, featureless area, you may need route-marking materials, particularly if the weather outlook is marginal. Be sure to carry such materials if your route plan indicates a possible need for them. If off-trail travel is involved, measure compass bearings and determine UTM or latitude/longitude coordinates of crucial locations at home before the trip and write them down in a notebook or note them on the edge of the map. Write down and discuss your route plan with other members of the party, so the party is not solely dependent on one person for all route decisions. You might consider requiring all party members (or at least children or inexperienced persons) to carry whistles.

Another thing you should do before the trip is to always tell a responsible person where you are going, what route you are taking, and when you plan on returning. This will not prevent you from getting lost. But if you *do* run into trouble, the authorities will know to look for you—and where to look. This one bit of preparation is an easy but essential task that could save your life. If, after leaving home and starting your trek, you wish to change your plans and select some alternate destination or route, you should seriously consider the consequences of doing so. Searchers will be looking in the wrong place if they do not know of your change in plans.

Always make sure that every member of the party carries adequate food, clothing, and other supplies (see "Survival," at the end of this chapter). In the event of any emergency, each person should have enough food and clothing to survive at least overnight, and perhaps several days, if necessary, while waiting for search-and-rescue personnel to arrive. Every party member should carry a map of the area and a compass, in case he or she becomes separated from the group.

During the Trip

Get off on the right foot by making sure that everyone understands the route and the route plan. Discuss the route and make contingency plans in case the party becomes separated. Be sure to save a GPS position at the trailhead or other location at the start of the trip and ensure that it is a solid 3-D position that makes sense to you. Once you are confident in this position, save it as a waypoint and jot down its name on your paper map.

Use handrails wherever possible. If you ever leave the security of your handrail, make a mental note of the fact that you are leaving it, and ask yourself what you will be following instead—a topographic feature, a contour line, a compass bearing, or anything else you can count on. You should not merely press onward without a clear idea of where you are headed or how to get back. At critical places, be sure to turn on your GPS receiver, establish your position, confirm that the position makes sense, locate it on your paper map, and save it as a GPS waypoint.

If you have a large group, do not let the group get too spread out. Agree ahead of time on places to stop and wait for everyone to catch up. If the group includes children or inexperienced persons, keep them in sight at all times. Assign a responsible, experienced person to be the rear guard, or sweep, to ensure that no straggler will be left behind.

Anticipate the Return Trip

The route always looks amazingly different on the way back to the starting point. Avoid surprises and confusion by glancing over your shoulder often, particularly at key route junctions, to see what the route should look like on the return. If you cannot keep track of it all, jot down times, elevations, landmarks, and so on in a small notebook. A few cryptic words, such as "7600, hit ridge," can save you a lot of grief on the return. It will remind you that when the party has dropped to 7600 feet as indicated on your altimeter, it is time to leave the ridge and start down the slope to your starting point. This is often faster than acquiring a GPS position and verifying its accuracy. You may merely plan on following the directions displayed on your GPS receiver, but remember to avoid complete dependence on it. What would you do if your batteries failed, or if you lost the receiver? You should always be able to return to your starting point using only map, compass, and topography.

Think

Your brain is your most important navigational tool, a fact often over-looked amid our reliance on compasses, altimeters, GPS receivers, and smart devices. As the party heads toward its destination, keep asking yourself questions: How will we recognize this important spot on our return? What would we do if the trip leader became incapacitated? Are we all placing our navigational reliance on one person? Could I find my way back alone if I had to? Would we be able to find our way back in a whiteout or in darkness, or if snow covered our tracks? Should we be marking the route right now? Could we get back if the GPS receiver failed, was damaged or lost, or if its batteries died? Ask the questions as you go, and act on your answers.

Mark the Route if Necessary

There are times when it may be best to physically mark the route going in so you can find it again on the way out. This situation can occur when the route passes over snowfields or glaciers during changeable weather, in heavy forest, or when fog threatens to hide landmarks. On snow, climbers use thin bamboo wands with little flags to mark the path. In the forest, plastic surveyor's tape is sometimes tied to branches to show the route, but we discourage its use due to its perma-nence since we always endeavor to leave no trace. From an ecological standpoint, toilet paper is the best marker, because it will disintegrate during the next rainfall. Use toilet paper only if you are assured of good weather. If not, use brightly colored crepe paper in thin rolls. It will survive the next storm, but it will most likely disintegrate during the winter.

Rock cairns appear here and there as markers, sometimes dotting an entire route and at other times signaling the point where a route changes direction. These heaps of rock are another imposition on the landscape, and they can create confusion for any traveler but the one who put them together—so do not build them. If there ever comes a time when you decide you must, then do so, but tear them down on the way out. (As the adage goes, "Take only pictures; leave only footprints.")

Keep Track

As the trip goes on, it may be helpful to mark your progress on the map. Keep yourself oriented so that at any time you can point out your actual position to within about a half mile (about 1 km) on the map.

With a watch and a notebook (or a really good memory), you can monitor your rate of progress on any outing. Always make sure to note your starting time as well as the times when you reach important streams, ridges, trail junctions, and other points along the route.

If it begins to look as though your party could become trapped in tricky terrain during darkness, you may decide to change your plans and call it a day and return home or set up camp.

Turnaround Time

Every wilderness trip, however sublime its objective, should have an agreed-upon turnaround time: the time of day by which you should stop and head back, and still have time to get back to the trailhead or camp with a comfortable amount of daylight.

At Your Destination

Your destination is the place to make final plans for the return, a journey often responsible for many more routefinding problems than on the way in. Ensure that all in your party understand the route plan, and stress the importance of keeping the party together on the return. Some may want to race ahead while others may lag behind. Turn on your GPS receiver, get a position fix, and save it. Then ask it to GO to the way-point of the trailhead or other starting point, and note the direction and distance to that waypoint. Set that direction on your compass and leave it there. If you lose the way to that place, you can simply take out your GPS device and find the general direction to that waypoint at any time.

During the Return Trip

As on the trip in, everyone needs to maintain a good sense of the route and how it relates to the map. Stay together, do not rush, and be even more careful if you are taking a different return route. If you ever get off track and are unsure of the direction to go, *stop!* Take out your GPS receiver, let it obtain a solid 3-D position fix, and find that position on your paper map. Tell it to GO to the next important waypoint on your route plan. Note the distance and direction to that place, set the direction on your compass, and use your compass to follow that bearing. Turn your receiver off and place it in a safe, secure place.

If it is getting late and you are in a hurry, you might not wish to keep turning your GPS receiver on and off and waiting for a position fix every time you want to know which direction to go. In this case, assuming that you have a sufficient supply of fresh batteries, you can keep the receiver on all the way back to your starting point, using the receiver's backtrack feature. Just be aware of the fact that you are draining your batteries by doing so.

CELL PHONES

Some hopelessly lost parties have been found by rescuers when they dialed 911 on their cell phones. It might be a good idea to carry yours into the wilderness as an added precaution. But mobile phones do not always work in all terrain or in all locations. They must be able to transmit and receive signals to and from the nearest cell tower, which might be out of range for many areas in the wilderness. Battery life is limited, and the signals can sometimes be blocked by mountains or other topographic features. So even if you do carry a cell phone, you should never consider it to be a dependable way of being found if you are lost. Take all the necessary steps to avoid getting lost, as described earlier in this chapter, and be completely self-reliant, since help might not be just a phone call away.

SMS messages may transfer more reliably than voice communications in weak cell areas, but it is possible that your SMS message will be only partially sent, therefore confusing the recipient.

"Triangulation" by "pinging" to find the distance from a cellular phone to two or more cell towers is occasionally used to determine the position of a lost hiker or other wilderness traveler. This method is of only limited usefulness, since it often leads rescuers to an unacceptably large search area if only one cell tower is within range. Furthermore, the use of this method is impossible if there is no cell tower within range of the user—a situation that often exists in the wilderness.

WHAT IF YOU *DO* GET LOST?

Good wilderness travelers are never truly lost—but having learned humility through years of experience, they always carry enough food, clothing, batteries, and bivouac gear to get them through hours or even days of temporary confusion.

What If Your Party Is Lost?

The first rule is to *stop*. In fact, even if you *think* you might not be where you should be, *stop!* Resist the temptation to press onward. The moment you are ever unsure of your position, you should stop. Try to determine where you are. Keep your wits about you and do not forget what you have learned about the GPS receiver and the map and compass. Study the shape of the terrain and try to associate it with the map to find out where you are. Take out your GPS receiver and turn it on. Let it acquire a good 3-D position fix, and ask it to GO to the waypoint that is your next or final destination. Set the indicated bearing on your compass, and find out which way that direction is. If these suggestions do not work, then try to figure out the last time you *did* know your exact location. If that spot is fairly close, retrace your steps and get back on route. But if that spot is hours back, you might decide instead to head toward the baseline. If it begins to look as though darkness will fall before you can get back, you might have to bivouac for the night. If so, start looking for an adequate place, with water and shelter if possible, well before dark.

Lost and Alone

Being lost in a party is bad enough, but it is even worse when an individual is separated from the rest of the party. For this reason, always try to keep everyone together. If you ever notice that someone is missing, the entire party should stop, stay together, shout, and listen for answering shouts. If party members carry whistles, you can sound yours and listen for answering sounds. It is generally understood that three of anything (light flashes, whistles, or other sounds) indicates injury, illness, or other forms of distress.

If you find yourself lost, *stop*. Look around for other members of the party, shout, and listen for answering shouts. Sound your whistle if you have one. If the only answer is silence, sit down, calm down, and combat terror with reason.

Once you have calmed down, look at your map in an attempt to determine your location, and plan a route home in case you do not connect with the rest of the party. Take out your GPS receiver and let it acquire a position fix. Ensure that it is a valid 3-D position, and read the coordinates off the screen. Find that location on the map. Then ask it to GO to your destination—the waypoint you took at the start of the trip or your next destination in your route.

If it begins to look as though you will not be able to get to your destination before dark, prepare for the night by finding water and shelter. Staying busy will raise your spirits. Try singing (no matter how bad a singer you are) so you will have something to do and so that any searchers will have something to hear. Get out in the open if possible—such as in a clearing or a meadow—and spread out brightly colored clothing, tarps, or other objects to make it easier for airborne searchers to find you.

It is possible that you will be reunited with your group by morning. If not, fight panic. After a night alone, you may decide to hike out to a baseline feature—a ridge or stream or highway—that you picked out before the trip, or to travel in the direction indicated by your GPS receiver. If the terrain is too difficult to travel alone, it might be better to concentrate on letting yourself be found. It is far easier for rescuers to find a lost person who stays in one place, out in the open, and who whistles or shouts periodically, than one who thrashes on in hysterical hope, one step ahead of the rescue party.

The decision to forge ahead or to stay put is strongly influenced by whether or not anyone knows you are missing, and where to look for you. If you are traveling alone, or if your entire party is lost, and no one knows you are missing or where you had planned to go, you have no choice but to try to find your way back, even if this involves difficult travel. If, on the other hand, someone responsible expects you back at a certain time and knows where you were planning to go and what route you had planned on taking, then you have the option of staying put, making yourself visible, and concentrating on survival while waiting for a search party to find you.

SURVIVAL

Your chances for survival depend on how well equipped you are. Numerous stories of survival and tragedy start with statements such as, "I was sure glad I had my ____," or "Too bad they did not bring a ____." Over the years these crucial items of gear have developed into a codified list known as *The Ten Essentials: A Systems Approach.*

1. **Navigation system:** This contains, as a minimum, a topographic map of the area and a compass. It might also include an altimeter, a GPS receiver, a whistle, and route-marking materials.
2. **Sun protection:** Sunglasses and sunscreen.
3. **Insulation:** Enough extra clothing to survive the most severe night that you can expect in the area you will be visiting.
4. **Illumination system:** A flashlight or headlamp, plus spare batteries and a spare bulb. Consider carrying a flashlight that uses the same kind of batteries as your GPS receiver, so that your spare batteries can be used for either.
5. **First-aid supplies:** Including any prescription medications that you take on a daily basis, in case you do not make it back home in time for the next dose.
6. **Fire system:** Matches in a waterproof case, firestarter, and stove fuel if you are carrying a stove.
7. **Repair kit and tools:** At a minimum, a good, multi-bladed knife. Add other tools depending on what equipment you might need to maintain.

8. **Nutrition:** In addition to snacks for the day, carry enough extra food to survive for at least an additional day longer than planned.
9. **Hydration system:** Adequate water plus a water purification method that will keep you in potable water for a week or more, if necessary.
10. **Emergency shelter:** A lightweight plastic tube tent, for example.

Always consider the possibility that one member of your party might become separated from the rest of the group and will depend totally on his or her own equipment and skill for survival. It is therefore essential for *each person* to carry adequate food and equipment. It is equally important that each person in the party have the knowledge and skill to use all the necessary equipment (including the map, compass, and the GPS receiver if they have one), rather than always relying on the skills of another. If someone gets lost, having the proper equipment and skills may make the difference between tragedy and a graceful recovery from the experience.

The Future of GPS

Whatever GPS technology improvements the future may bring, we still recommend that you always carry a good paper topo map or marine chart of your intended area of travel, along with a stand-alone baseplate compass. The GPS receiver is a marvelous supplemental navigational tool to have with you on any wilderness experience, but it is no substitute for traditional map and compass techniques or common sense. Neither your paper topo map or chart, nor your traditional baseplate compass will ever become useless as a result of having exhausted its batteries.

Today the use of GPS technology is pervasive in many aspects of everyday life. Technological advances in LCD displays, microelectronics, and satellite technology have greatly enhanced GPS functionality, and improvements in battery technology have increased the time required before battery replacement or recharging.

New models, or *blocks*, of GPS satellites have been developed over the past few years, and Block IIF satellites are now being brought online. Another wave of Block III satellites is currently in development. These new satellites will provide stronger GPS signals, improved accuracy, and enhanced reliability. Future improvements in battery and electronics technology, as well as better displays, promise to improve GPS usability even more. At the same time, as more and more users are added, mass production continues to bring the cost of GPS receivers down. GPS technology is getting better and better all the time.

The Global Positioning System is an incredible technology, but it has yet to fully realize its greatest potential for the wilderness traveler. In perfect conditions, GPS units are remarkably reliable as far as

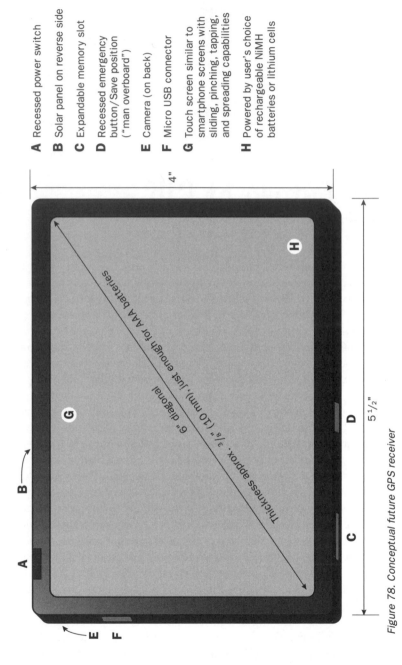

A Recessed power switch

B Solar panel on reverse side

C Expandable memory slot

D Recessed emergency button/Save position ("man overboard")

E Camera (on back)

F Micro USB connector

G Touch screen similar to smartphone screens with sliding, pinching, tapping, and spreading capabilities

H Powered by user's choice of rechargeable NiMH batteries or lithium cells

4"

5 1/2"

6" diagonal

Thickness approx. ³/₈" (10 mm), just enough for AAA batteries

Figure 78. Conceptual future GPS receiver

signal detection goes, but in many instances the user interface is still remarkably clunky. Even when touch-screen technology is used in GPS receivers, most currently used display screens are just too small (necessarily so, currently, to conserve battery power), which largely limits the big picture view, especially when compared to a traditional paper map. Compounding this is the relative antiquity of many GPS devices, such as the use of joysticks and physical buttons that seem awkward in our increasingly touch-screen world. Smartphone technology is advancing rapidly, yet the data stream for maps is unavailable when the Wi-Fi or cellular network is not available.

Regardless of advances in GPS technology that occur in the future, the processes of determining your exact point position and of navigation and routefinding cannot be achieved through the blind use of the latest technology. Imagine discovering that you are lost and turning on your smart device only to discover that you have merely 3 percent of your battery life remaining because you accidentally left an app running that tells you traffic conditions near your home. Or imagine that you fire up your GPS receiver when you are lost, only to recall that you never did figure out how to switch from latitude/longitude to the UTM coordinate system. Even though you are carrying a good paper map, you really cannot pinpoint your location to any real degree of accuracy using the lat/long system. Point position determination, navigation, and routefinding are not rooted in electronics technology but rather in experience and knowledge of traditional map and compass techniques.

Lastly, the authors challenge GPS device manufacturers to construct touch-screen GPS receivers with large displays that sip energy; have replaceable, readily available batteries (such as AA or AAA) or, at a minimum, field rechargeable batteries; perhaps with a solar array on the back of the device; and which come with detailed topo maps already installed. Seamless Bluetooth connectivity between the GPS device and the personal computer would also be a helpful feature. An example of such a (presently nonexistent) GPS receiver is shown in figure 78. It shows a GPS unit with a large six-inch touch screen with a solar panel array on the back, as well as a few other useful features. Perhaps your concept of an ideal GPS device differs from ours. If so, come up with your own ideas. Contact your GPS manufacturers and tell them what you want. Eventually, with enough input, they will respond, and future generations will benefit.

Appendix A

Interpreting and Using Maps and Charts

A map is a symbolic picture of a place. In convenient shorthand, it conveys a phenomenal amount of information in a form that is easy to understand and easy to carry. No one should venture into the wilderness without a paper map or chart of the area, or without the skills required to interpret and thoroughly understand it, whether you have a GPS receiver or not. Note that what follows is only a brief overview of map and compass essentials. Refer to our other book, *Wilderness Navigation: Finding Your Way Using Map, Compass, Altimeter, and GPS*, for complete information and helpful tips.

MAP AND CHART SCALES AND TERMINOLOGY

Topographic maps and nautical charts are the best of all maps for wilderness travelers. Topographic maps depict the shape of the earth's surface by showing contour lines that represent constant elevations referenced to sea level. Nautical charts show coastlines, navigation hazards, navigation aids, shipping lanes, and other information of interest to the marine navigator. Some are produced by government agencies, such as the US Geological Survey, US Coast and Geodetic Survey, National Oceanic and Atmospheric Administration, and Canadian Hydrographic Service, whereas others are printed by private companies.

Latitude and Longitude

The distance around our planet is divided into 360 units called *degrees*. A measurement east or west is called *longitude*. A measurement north or south is called *latitude*. Longitude is measured from 0° to 180°, both east and west, starting at the Greenwich meridian near London, England. Latitude is measured from 0° to 90°, north and south, starting from the equator. New York City, for example, is situated at about 74 degrees west longitude and 41 degrees north latitude (74° W and 41° N).

Each degree is divided into sixty units called *minutes* (designated with a ' symbol), and each minute is further subdivided into sixty *seconds* (designated with a " symbol). On a map, a latitude of 46 degrees, 53 minutes, and 15 seconds north would be written 46°53'15"N.

One feature of this system is that one minute of latitude is equal to one nautical mile (6076 feet or 1852 meters). Since there are 60 seconds in a minute, this means that one second of latitude corresponds to 101 feet (34 yards or 31 meters).

When using land navigation techniques with topographic maps, the UTM coordinate system is easier and more accurate than the latitude and longitude system. Most marine charts, however, use the latitude/longitude system, since UTM lines and coordinates are not present. Marine charts have special scales printed along the edges that facilitate the use of this system, provided that you know how to use them.

An example is shown in figure 79 (next page). Latitude is shown along the left and right edges of the chart, and longitude is shown along the top and bottom. Note that each minute of latitude and longitude is divided into ten small divisions. Since one minute equals 60 seconds, the smallest division is therefore 6 seconds (0.10 minute) on this chart. (This relationship is valid for charts with a scale of 1:80,000, a commonly used scale in many areas. However, many different scales are used on marine charts, so the number of seconds or minutes for the smallest division will vary from one chart to another with a different scale.)

The point identified as "Northeast Pt." in figure 79 has latitude 49 degrees, 42 minutes, and 36 seconds (49°42'36") and longitude 124°21'24". You can easily find these coordinates by drawing horizontal and vertical lines through the point of interest to the edges of the chart, as shown. The numbers are interpolated from where these lines intersect the scales on the edges of the chart.

It is easier to interpolate between marked divisions if you use degrees, minutes, and decimal minutes. In the above example, since each minute is divided into ten subdivisions, the smallest division equals 0.10 minute. The point described in this example is seen to have latitude 49°42.6' North and longitude 124°21.4' West. If you use this method you should set your GPS unit's coordinate system to degrees, minutes, and decimal minutes (DD M.MM).

Scales

The *scale* of any map or chart is the ratio between dimensions on the paper map and those in the actual field. For example, a scale of 1 to 24,000 (1:24,000, the USGS standard for most of the United States)

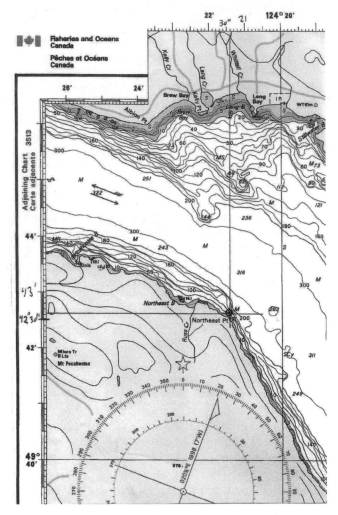

Figure 79. Marine navigation chart showing latitude/longitude coordinates

means that one unit on the map represents 24,000 units in the field. With 12 inches to the foot, this means one inch on the map corresponds to 2000 feet, or about 0.38 mile (0.61 kilometer). It also means that 1 mile in the field is represented as 2.6 inches on the map. For the rest of the world, where metric units are used, a scale of 1:25,000 is commonly used. These scales provide a great amount of detail, usually sufficient for any kind of off-trail wilderness travel. These are the scales that you should look for in selecting any map-displaying GPS receiver. Topographic maps with a scale of 1:24,000 or 1:25,000 are preloaded into some GPS receivers and can be downloaded onto some others.

Another commonly used scale is the 1:100,000, in which 1 inch on the map corresponds to 100,000 inches in the field, or 8333 feet or 1.6 miles (2.5 kilometers). This scale gives far less detail than the 1:24,000 scale. Topographic maps with the 1:100,000 scale are preloaded into many types of GPS receivers and are adequate for many types of activities, such as trail hiking. However, when venturing off-trail, most users prefer the 1:24,000 or 1:25,000 scale due to their superior detail. When buying a receiver with preloaded maps, or considering the purchase of micro-SD cards with topo maps, it is important to choose a map scale appropriate to your activities.

The type of USGS map most commonly used by wilderness travelers covers an area of 7.5 minutes (that is, ⅛ degree) of latitude by 7.5 minutes of longitude. These maps are known as the *7.5-minute series*. An older type of USGS map covers an area of 15 minutes (that is, ¼ degree) of latitude by 15 minutes of longitude. These maps are part of what is called the *15-minute series*.

In the USGS 7.5-minute series, the scale is 1:24,000. Each map covers an area of approximately 6 by 9 miles (9 by 14 km). In the 15-minute series, the scale is 1:62,500, or about 1 inch to 1 mile (1.6 cm to 1 km), and each map covers an area of about 12 by 18 miles (18 by 28 km). Off-trail travelers prefer the 7.5-minute maps because of the greater detail. The 7.5-minute map is the standard for the continental United States and Hawaii. The 15-minute map is the standard only for Alaska; its scale is 1:63,360, or exactly 1 inch to 1 mile.

HOW TO READ TOPOGRAPHIC MAPS

A map's language is easy to learn and pays immediate rewards to any wilderness traveler. Some of this language is in words, but most of it is in the form of symbols. Each map is referred to as a quadrangle (or quad) and covers an area bounded on the north and south by latitude lines that differ by an amount equal to the map series (7.5 minutes or 15 minutes), and on the east and west by longitude lines that differ by the same amount, except for Alaska. Each quadrangle is given the name of a prominent topographic or human-made feature in the area.

Declination Information and North–South Reference Lines

The margins of USGS maps contain important information, such as the date of publication and revision, the names of maps of adjacent areas, contour intervals, and map scales. The margin also gives the area's magnetic declination, which is the difference between true north and magnetic north. Declination is extremely important and will be discussed in appendix B. USGS topographic maps printed in 1988 or later, such as that shown in figure 80A, have a statement such as "1990 Magnetic North Declination 20° EAST." Maps printed before 1988 usually have a declination diagram printed near the lower left corner (see fig. 80B). The star indicates true north and the "MN" indicates magnetic north. The difference between these two is the magnetic declination.

Depending on the map's date of revision, there may or may not be UTM lines printed on the map. Maps printed in 1988 or later usually have a grid of black lines representing the 1000-meter intervals of the UTM grid (see fig. 80A). This grid is usually slightly offset from true north. The amount of this offset is given by a statement in the lower left corner of the map such as "UTM GRID DECLINATION 0°14' WEST." The UTM grid can be used as north–south lines for use with a compass, as will be explained in appendix B. UTM is also very helpful when using a GPS receiver.

If UTM lines do not truly run north–south, then you should draw in your own north–south lines. Put your map on a table and place one long edge of a yardstick (or meter stick or other long straightedge) along the left margin of the map. Draw a line along the other side of the stick, and then move the stick over to the line you have just drawn and draw another line, and another, and so on until you reach the center of the map. Then place the stick along the right margin of the map and repeat the procedure. This way, you will have a set of north–south lines that are truly north-south. This will help you achieve accuracy in measuring and plotting bearings on the map using your compass, as explained in appendix B.

On maps printed prior to 1988, UTM lines are usually not shown. However, there are faint "tick" marks along the edges of such maps showing the locations of the 1000-meter lines (see fig. 80B). The declination diagrams for these maps usually have a line to GN, meaning grid north. This is the offset of the UTM grid from true north. You can connect these tick marks on your table at home using a meter stick or a yardstick to place a UTM grid on the map. You can also use these as north–south reference lines. However, if the amount of difference between true north and grid north is greater than 1 degree, then you should draw in your own north–south lines parallel with the edges of the map, as described above.

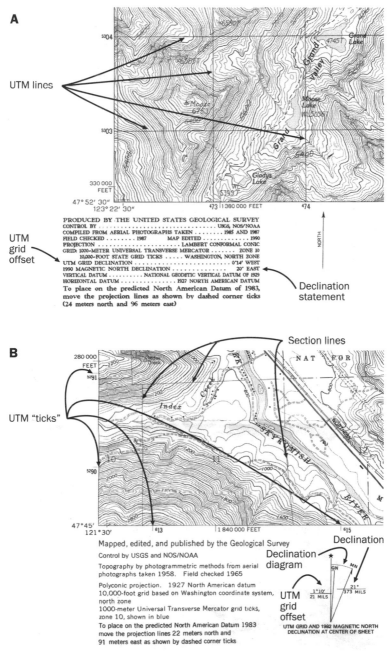

Figure 80. Lower left corner of USGS topographic maps: (A) 1988 or later, (B) earlier than 1988

What the Colors Mean

Colors on a USGS topographic map have specific meanings:

Red: Major roads and survey information.

Blue: Rivers, lakes, springs, waterfalls, and other water features.

Black: Minor roads, trails, railroads, buildings, bench marks, latitude and longitude lines, UTM coordinates and lines, and other features not part of the natural environment.

Green: Areas of heavy forest. Solid green marks a forested area, while mottled green indicates scrub vegetation.

White: The color of the paper on which the map is printed; it can have a variety of meanings, depending on the terrain.

    White with blue contour lines: A glacier or permanent snowfield. The contour lines of glaciers and permanent snowfields are in solid blue, with their edges indicated by dashed blue lines. Elevations are shown in blue. Rope up for all glacier travel!

    White with brown contour lines: Any area without substantial forest, such as a high alpine area, a clear-cut, a rock slide, an avalanche gully, or a meadow. Study the map for other clues.

Brown: Contour lines and elevations, everywhere except on glaciers and permanent snowfields.

Purple: Partial revision of an existing map.

Translating Contour Lines

The heart of a topographic map is its overlay of contour lines, each line indicating a constant elevation as it follows the shape of the landscape. A map's contour interval is the difference in elevation between two adjacent contour lines. The contour interval is clearly printed at the bottom of the map. Every fifth contour line, called an *index contour,* is printed darker than the other lines and is labeled with the elevation.

One of the most important bits of information a topographic map reveals is whether you will be traveling uphill or downhill. If the route crosses lines of increasingly higher elevation, you will be going uphill. If it crosses lines of decreasing elevation, the route is downhill. Flat or sidehill travel is indicated by a route that crosses no lines, remaining within a single contour interval.

Topographic maps also show cliffs, passes, summits, and other features. Main features depicted by contour lines include the following (see fig. 81):

    1. **Nearly flat area:** No contour lines at all.

    2. **Gentle slope:** Widely spaced contour lines.

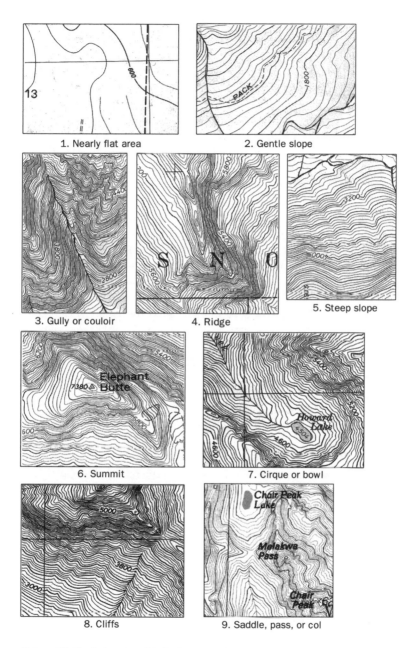

1. Nearly flat area   2. Gentle slope

3. Gully or couloir   4. Ridge   5. Steep slope

6. Summit   7. Cirque or bowl

8. Cliffs   9. Saddle, pass, or col

Figure 81. Basic topographic features

3. **Gully or couloir:** Contour lines in a pattern of **U**s for gentle, rounded valleys or gullies; **V**s for sharp valleys and gullies. The **U**s and **V**s point uphill, in the direction of higher elevation.

4. **Ridge:** Contour lines in a pattern of **U**s for gentle, rounded ridges; **V**s for sharp ridges. The **U**s and **V**s point downhill, in the direction of lower elevation.

5. **Steep slopes:** Closely spaced contour lines.

6. **Summit:** A concentric pattern of contour lines, with the summit being the innermost and highest ring. Peaks are also often indicated by **X**s, elevations, bench marks (BMs), or a triangle symbol.

7. **Cirque or bowl:** Patterns of contour lines forming a semicircle (or as much as three-quarters of a circle), rising from a low spot in the center to form a natural amphitheater at the head of a valley.

8. **Cliffs:** Contour lines extremely close together or touching.

9. **Saddle, pass, or col:** An hourglass shape, with higher contour lines on two sides, indicating a low point on a ridge.

As you travel in the wilderness, be sure to observe the terrain and its depiction on the map. Note all the topographic features—such as ridges, gullies, streams, and summits—as you pass them. This helps you to maintain a close estimate of exactly where you are (orientation) and helps you become an expert map reader. You will get better and better at interpreting these lines by comparing actual terrain with its representation on the map (see fig. 82). Your goal should be to glance at a topographic map and have a sharp mental image of just what the place will look like.

USING AN ALTIMETER AND MAP TOGETHER

In mountainous terrain, a GPS receiver or altimeter watch indicates the elevation above sea level. Often this knowledge, along with features shown on a topographic map, can help to pinpoint your position on the map. For example, if a trail is steadily gaining elevation as it climbs toward the top of a hill or mountain, a glance at the altimeter will indicate your elevation to within about a hundred feet (30 meters), or even closer. Finding the place on the map where the trail crosses a contour line at that elevation indicates your likely position on the trail.

The barometric altimeter responds to changes in barometric pressure, which decreases at a predictable rate with increasing elevation. It therefore responds not only to altitude but also to changes in barometric pressure, which is strongly influenced by the weather. For this reason, when going on any trip where you want to use the altimeter,

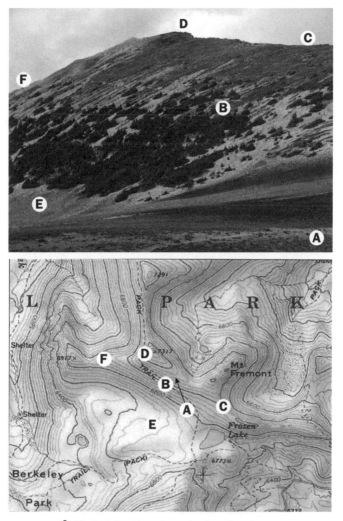

A Photo taken from here, in direction shown
B Trail along hillside with moderate slope
C Ridge crest
D Minor summit along ridge crest
E Nearly flat area below light forest
F Skyline ridge

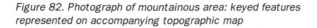

Figure 82. Photograph of mountainous area: keyed features represented on accompanying topographic map

it is important for you to first set the altimeter to the correct elevation at your starting point, such as a trailhead, which you can find on the map. During the course of the trip, if you reach another point of known elevation, such as a lake or peak whose elevation is printed on the map, you can check your altimeter to ensure that it is correct, or you can reset it if it is not. Even the best of altimeters frequently display elevations that are wrong by as much as a hundred feet (30 meters), not because of any problem with the altimeter, but merely due to changes in barometric pressure as weather conditions change.

GPS receivers usually display altitude as well as horizontal position, and this information can be used instead of an altimeter reading. Altitude displayed on a GPS receiver is not affected by weather-related changes in barometric pressure, but GPS-indicated altitude is not quite as accurate as the horizontal position displayed on the receiver. Altitude errors of up to 100 feet (30 meters) are common when using GPS receivers.

THE UNIVERSAL TRANSVERSE MERCATOR (UTM) COORDINATE SYSTEM

The traditional method of defining position information on this planet is that of latitude/longitude. It is the primary method of locating any given position on nautical charts for marine applications. However, it is awkward and difficult to use with accuracy when using USGS or comparable topographic maps because such maps display latitude and longitude coordinates for only a few places on each map. Also the east–west distance for any given change in longitude varies from one latitude to another because the lines of longitude converge at the poles. The latitude/longitude coordinate system is usually the default system on GPS receivers, and changing it to UTM is an important part of setting up a newly obtained receiver for use with USGS topo maps.

The UTM system is a grid of north–south and east–west lines at intervals of 1000 meters (3281 feet or 0.6214 mile). This is far more precise than the latitude/longitude system, because USGS maps only identify latitude and longitude coordinates every 2.5 minutes, that is, approximately every 2 to 3 miles (3 to 4 km). Without using a scale or ruler, you can usually eyeball your UTM position to within about 100 meters (about 300 feet), which is often close enough to get you to within sight of your objective. In the UTM system, the Earth is divided into sixty *zones* that are each 6 degrees wide. The zone number is printed in the lower left corner of USGS maps (see fig. 83).

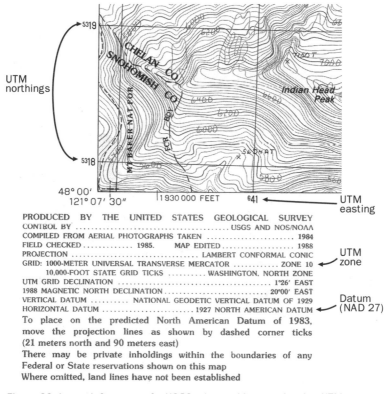

48° 00'
121° 07' 30"   1 930 000 FEET   **6**41 ← UTM easting

PRODUCED BY THE UNITED STATES GEOLOGICAL SURVEY
CONTROL BY .... USGS AND NOS/NOAA
COMPILED FROM AERIAL PHOTOGRAPHS TAKEN 1984
FIELD CHECKED .... 1985.   MAP EDITED 1988
PROJECTION .... LAMBERT CONFORMAL CONIC
GRID: 1000-METER UNIVERSAL TRANSVERSE MERCATOR .... ZONE 10 ← UTM zone
    10,000-FOOT STATE GRID TICKS .... WASHINGTON, NORTH ZONE
UTM GRID DECLINATION .... 1°26' EAST
1988 MAGNETIC NORTH DECLINATION .... 20°00' EAST
VERTICAL DATUM .... NATIONAL GEODETIC VERTICAL DATUM OF 1929   Datum
HORIZONTAL DATUM .... 1927 NORTH AMERICAN DATUM ← (NAD 27)
To place on the predicted North American Datum of 1983,
move the projection lines as shown by dashed corner ticks
(21 meters north and 90 meters east)
There may be private inholdings within the boundaries of any
Federal or State reservations shown on this map
Where omitted, land lines have not been established

Figure 83. Lower left corner of a USGS topographic map showing UTM zone and horizontal datum. UTM partial eastings and northings also shown.

Identifying Displayed GPS Position on a USGS Topo Map

For example, suppose you are climbing Glacier Peak, and clouds obscure all visibility. You reach a summit but are not sure whether it is the true summit of Glacier Peak (see fig. 84). You turn on your GPS receiver and let it acquire a position. The UTM numbers displayed on the screen of your GPS receiver are as follows:

10 6 40 612E

53 29 491N

The top number is called an *easting*, which indicates the number of meters east of an imaginary reference line for your area. The number "10" is the *zone* number. The numbers "6 40 612E" indicate that your position is 640,612 meters east of the reference line for that zone. In figure 84, you can find the number "6 40 000mE" along the top edge of the map. This

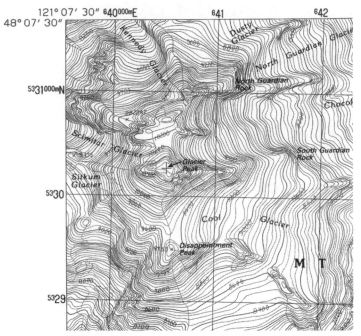

Figure 84. Close-up of USGS map showing Glacier Peak summit area

is the *full easting* (except for the zone number). To the right of this is the number 6 41. This is a *partial easting*, with the "000" meters omitted. You can see that the number "6 40 612E" on the screen of the GPS receiver is approximately six-tenths of the way between 6 40 000 and 6 41 000. Your east–west position is therefore about six-tenths of the way between the 6 40 000 and the 6 41 000 lines.

Along the left edge of the map is the number "53 31 000mN." This is the *full northing*, which indicates that this point is 5,331,000 meters north of the equator. Below this is a line labeled "53 30," and another labeled "53 29." These are *partial northings*, with the "000" meters omitted. The second set of numbers displayed on the GPS receiver is 53 29 491N. This is a horizontal line about halfway between 53 29 and 53 30. The point where the easting and the northing lines intersect is your *point position*. Finding this point in figure 84 shows that you are on Disappointment Peak, not Glacier Peak.

How to Get Better Precision

If you have difficulty eyeballing distances between UTM coordinate lines, there are several types of special rulers and other measuring devices that you can use. You can purchase small plastic scales to read UTM coordinates on 1:24,000-scale (7.5-minute) maps, but this means carrying one more piece of special equipment. Alternatively, you can cut the scale off the bottom of a map you no longer need (or photocopy a portion of a topo map) and glue it to a piece of heavy paper or cardboard, as shown in figure 85.

Figure 85. Homemade map scale

Some compasses (fig. 86) are equipped with special scales to locate your position on 1:24,000-scale maps; some of these have "GPS" in their model numbers. Other compasses have "roamer" (sometimes spelled "romer") scales for use with either 1:24,000- or 1:25,000-scale maps. Since USGS 7.5-minute maps have a scale of 1:24,000, that is the scale you should use. However, if your compass has a roamer scale for use with 1:25,000-scale maps, it is close

Figure 86. Compass with roamer scales

enough to 1:24,000 that you can use it anyway, with only minimal error.

Reading UTM Position off Topo Maps

You can also use UTM for situations in which you can identify your desired destination on the map but cannot actually see it in the field. You can read the UTM position of the destination off the map and then enter it into the GPS receiver as a waypoint.

Going back to the Glacier Peak example shown in figure 84, suppose you wish to find the route from Disappointment Peak to the summit of Glacier Peak. From the map, you can see that the summit of Glacier Peak is about halfway between the eastings of 6 40 000 and 6 41 000, so you could estimate the easting as 10 6 40 500 (the zone number in this example is still 10). You can also see that the summit is about three-tenths of the way between the northings of 53 30 000 and 53 31 000, so you can estimate the full northing to be 53 30 300N. You

Table 4. Latitude Bands and Ranges

Band	Range	Band	Range
C	72–80 South	N	0–8 North
D	64–72 South	P	8–16 North
E	56–64 South	Q	16–24 North
F	48–56 South	R	24–32 North
G	40–48 South	S	32–40 North
H	32–40 South	T	40–48 North
J	24–32 South	U	48–56 North
K	16–24 South	V	56–64 North
L	8–16 South	W	64–72 North
M	0–8 South	X	72–84 North

can then enter the UTM coordinates of 10 6 40 500E and 53 30 300N into the GPS receiver and define this position as a waypoint.

Latitude Bands

Some GPS receivers use a "latitude band" with UTM to indicate position relative to the equator (zero degrees). This system divides the earth into 8-degree-wide latitude bands from 80° S latitude to 84° N latitude (the northernmost band being a bit wider than the others). The bands are lettered from south to north, as shown in table 4. If the latitude band is used, the letter for that band is placed immediately after the zone number. In the Glacier Peak example above, the zone and latitude band would be labeled "10U", since the latitude is between 48 and 56 degrees north latitude. Some GPS receivers use latitude bands, and some do not.

Universal Polar Stereographic (UPS) Coordinate System

Due to distortion of the UTM grid lines near the poles, UTM is not defined north of 84° N or south of 80° S latitude. The area covered by UTM includes most of the world except Antarctica and arctic regions north of Alaska's north coast. In those areas you can use latitude and longitude or the Universal Polar Stereographic (UPS) grid instead. If you anticipate travel to any such areas, be sure to check the specifications to ensure that the receiver will support the UPS grid. Most receivers can handle both the UTM and UPS systems as well as the latitude/longitude system.

Appendix B

A compass is nothing more than a magnetized needle that responds to the earth's magnetic field. Compass makers have added a few things to this basic unit to make it easier to use. But stripped to the core, there is just that needle, aligned with the earth's magnetism, and from that we can figure out any direction.

TYPES OF BASEPLATE COMPASSES

The basic features (see fig. 87A) of a compass to be used for wilderness travel include:

- A freely rotating magnetic needle—one end is a different color (usually red) from the other so you can tell which end points to north.
- A circular, rotating housing, or capsule, for the needle—filled with a fluid that dampens (reduces) the vibrations of the needle, making readings more accurate.
- A dial around the circumference of the housing—preferably graduated clockwise in 2-degree increments from 0° to 360°.
- An orienting arrow and a set of parallel meridian lines—located below the needle.
- An index line—used to set and read bearings.
- A transparent, rectangular base plate for the entire unit, including a direction of travel line.

Optional features (see fig. 87B) available on some compasses include:

- An adjustable declination arrow—an easy, dependable way to correct for magnetic declination; well worth the added cost.
- A sighting mirror—another way to improve accuracy.
- A ruler—calibrated in inches or millimeters; used to measure short distances on a map.
- A clinometer—used to measure the angle of a slope in the field.
- A magnifying glass—used to help read closely spaced contour lines and other minute details on maps.

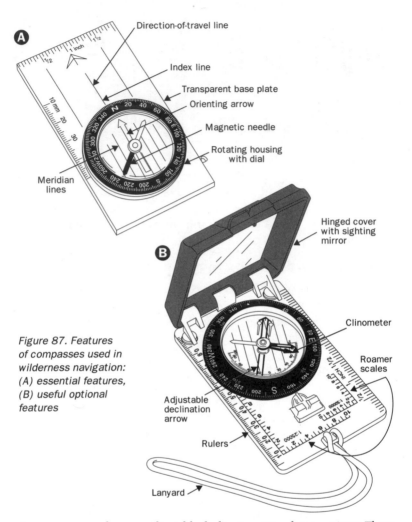

Figure 87. Features of compasses used in wilderness navigation: (A) essential features, (B) useful optional features

Some compasses have an adjustable declination arrow but no mirror. These cost a little more than the basic compass of figure 87A but considerably less than the full-featured compass of figure 87B. They offer a good compromise for someone who prefers the adjustable declination arrow but does not want to pay the added cost of the mirror.

BEARINGS IN THE FIELD

A *bearing* is the direction from one place to another, measured in degrees of angle with respect to an accepted reference line. This reference is the line to true north.

The round dial of a compass is divided into 360 degrees. The direction in degrees to each of the cardinal directions, going clockwise around the dial starting from the top, is north, 0° (the same as 360°); east, 90°; south, 180°; and west, 270° (see fig. 88).

The compass is used for two basic tasks regarding bearings:

1. **To take, or measure, bearings.** To take a bearing means to measure the direction from one point to another, either on a map or in the field.

2. **To plot, or follow, bearings.** To plot, or follow, a bearing means to set a certain bearing on the compass and then to plot out, or to follow, where that bearing points, either on the map or in the field.

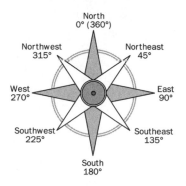

Figure 88. Cardinal directions and corresponding degree designations on compass

All bearings in the field are based on where the needle points. For the sake of simplicity, we will first ignore the effects of magnetic declination, a subject that will be taken up in the next section. Let us imagine that we are in central Missouri, where the declination is negligible.

To take (measure) a bearing in the field: Hold the compass in front of you and point the direction of travel line at the object whose bearing you want to find. Then rotate the compass housing until the pointed end of the orienting arrow is aligned with the north-seeking (usually red) end of the magnetic needle. (This process is sometimes referred to as "boxing the needle" or "getting the dog in the doghouse.") Read the bearing at the index line (fig. 89).

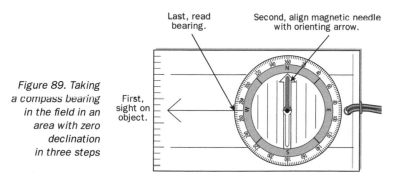

Figure 89. Taking a compass bearing in the field in an area with zero declination in three steps

Figure 90. Taking a bearing using a compass that does not have a mirror

Figure 91. Taking a bearing using a compass with a mirror

If the compass has no sighting mirror, hold it at or near arm's length and at or near waist level, with your arm straight at about a 45-degree angle from your body (see fig. 90). This is a compromise between sighting with the compass at eye level (sighting on your objective along the edge of the compass, without being able to see the compass needle or orienting arrow) or holding it straight down (being able to see the compass needle and arrow without parallax but losing sight of the objective).

With a sighting mirror, no such compromise is necessary. Fold the mirror back to a 45-degree angle and hold the compass at eye level, with the sight pointing at the object (see fig. 91). Observe the magnetic needle and the orienting arrow in the mirror as you rotate the housing to align the needle and the arrow. In either case, hold the compass level. Keep it away from metal objects, which can easily deflect the magnetic needle, giving you a false reading.

To follow (plot) a bearing in the field: Simply reverse the process you used to take a bearing. Rotate the compass housing until you have set the desired bearing at the index line, say 270° (west). Then hold the compass level in front of you, at roughly arm's length and waist height. Turn your entire body (including your feet) until the north-seeking end of the magnetic needle is aligned with the pointed end of the orienting arrow (i.e., box the needle). The direction of travel line is now pointing in whatever direction you have set at the index line, in this case west.

MAGNETIC DECLINATION

A compass needle is attracted to *magnetic* north, while most maps are printed with true north—the direction to the geographic north pole—at the top. This difference between the direction to true north and the direction to magnetic north, measured in degrees, is called *magnetic declination*. You will need to make a simple compass adjustment or modification to correct for declination.

Magnetic declination varies from place to place and over time. Always use the most current topographic map for your area. To find the amount and direction of declination for the map, look in the lower left corner on USGS topographic maps (see fig. 80, page 127).

The map of the United States shown in figure 92 will give you a fairly good idea of the declination in your area. The map is for 2015 and is valid for the time interval from 2010 to 2020. In figure 92, you can see that the line of zero declination runs through parts of Minnesota, Iowa, Missouri, Arkansas, Mississippi, and Louisiana. Along this line, the magnetic needle points in the same direction as the geographic north pole (true north), so no correction for declination is necessary. But in areas west of this line, the magnetic needle points somewhere to the east (to the right) of true north, so these areas are said to have *east declination*. It works just the opposite on the other side of the line of zero declination, such as on the East Coast of the United States. Here, the magnetic needle points somewhere to the west (left) of true north, so these areas are said to have *west declination*.

Figure 93 shows the declination for the state of Alaska in 2015, also valid for the time interval between 2010 and 2020.

Correcting for Declination

Consider a wilderness traveler in northern Utah, with a declination of 12° east. The true bearing is a measurement of the angle between the line to true north and the line to the objective, as shown in figure 94A. The magnetic needle, however, is pulled toward magnetic north, not true north. So instead it measures the angle between the line to magnetic north and the line to the objective. This "magnetic bearing" is 12° less than the true bearing. To get the true bearing, you could *add* 12° to the magnetic bearing.

As in Utah, travelers in all areas west of the zero declination line could add the declination to the magnetic bearing to get a true bearing. In central Colorado, for example, about 9° could be added. In western Washington State, you could add about 16°.

East of the zero declination line, the declination could be *subtracted* from the magnetic bearing to get the true bearing. In central New Hampshire, for example (see fig. 94B), the magnetic bearing is about 15° greater than the true bearing. To get a true bearing, the traveler in

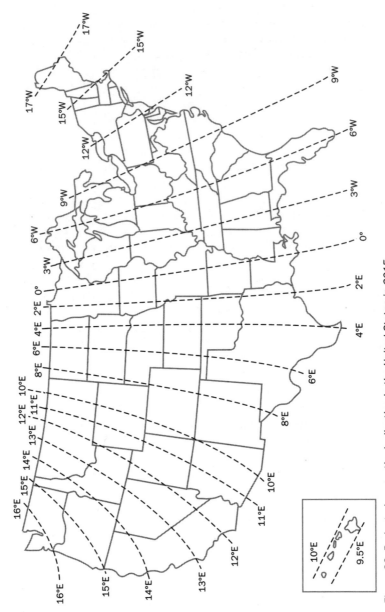

Figure 92. Projected magnetic declination in the United States in 2015

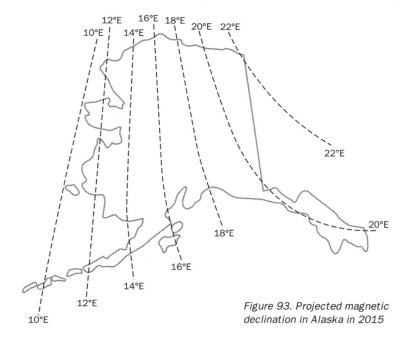

Figure 93. Projected magnetic declination in Alaska in 2015

New Hampshire could subtract the declination of 15° from the magnetic bearing.

A Better Way to Correct for Declination

Arithmetic correction for magnetic declination is very simple in theory but can be confusing in practice, and the wilderness is no place for mental arithmetic that can have serious consequences when you make a mistake. A more practical way to handle the minor complication of declination is to pay a little more for your compass and get one with an adjustable *declination arrow* instead of a fixed orienting arrow. By following the instructions supplied with the compass, you can easily set the declination arrow—usually by inserting a tiny screwdriver (often attached to the lanyard) into a small slot and turning it until the declination arrow points at the correct number of degrees east or west of the index line. Then the bearing that you read at the index line will automatically be the true bearing, and concern about a declination error is one worry you can leave at home. Compasses with adjustable declination arrows are sometimes called "set and forget" compasses.

If you have a compass with adjustable declination and set it for a declination of 12° east, as for northern Utah, then, once properly

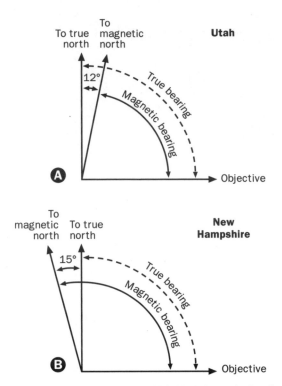

Figure 94. Magnetic and true bearings: (A) in Utah (east declination), (B) in New Hampshire (west declination)

adjusted, the pointed end of the declination arrow will point to 12°. In central New Hampshire, with a declination of 15° west, the correctly adjusted declination arrow will point to 345° (15° less than 360°).

On compasses without adjustable declination arrows, you can achieve the same effect by sticking a thin strip of tape to the bottom of the rotating housing to serve as a customized declination arrow. Trim the tape to a point, and apply it to the underside of the compass for the area where you will be traveling, as shown in figure 95.

In Utah, your taped declination arrow must point at 12° east (clockwise) from the 360-degree point (marked *N* for north) on the rotating dial (fig. 95A). In New Hampshire, the declination arrow must point at 15° west (counterclockwise) from the 360-degree mark (fig. 95B), or 345°. In the western part of Washington State, the declination arrow must point at 16° east (clockwise) from 360°. Note that this taped declination arrow is located exactly the same as the adjustable declination arrow described above.

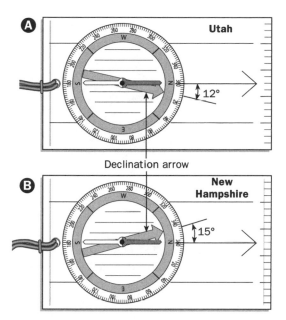

Figure 95. Compass declination corrections: (A) for an area west of the zero-declination line, (B) for an area east of the zero declination line

Note: If you travel to an area with different declination, you will have to change the declination correction.

To take a bearing in the field, follow the same procedure used in the earlier examples for Missouri. The only difference is that, from now on, you will align the magnetic needle with the *declination arrow* instead of with the orienting arrow. Always remember to align the north-seeking end of the magnetic needle with the pointed end of the declination arrow to box the needle.

BACK BEARINGS

A *back bearing* is the opposite direction of a bearing. Back bearings are often useful when you are trying to follow a certain bearing, and you want to check to see if you are still on the bearing line by taking a back bearing on your starting point. If your bearing is less than 180°, then you can find the back bearing by adding 180° to the original bearing. If your bearing is greater than 180°, then you can find the back bearing by subtracting 180° from the original bearing. For example, if you are traveling at a bearing of 90°, then the back bearing is 270°. Once you reach your destination, following the back bearing of 270° should get you back to your starting point.

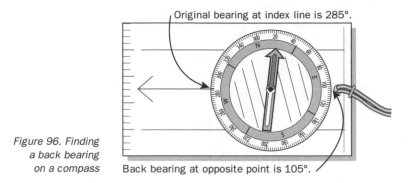

Original bearing at index line is 285°.

*Figure 96. Finding
a back bearing
on a compass*

Back bearing at opposite point is 105°.

One way to find a back bearing is to set your original bearing at the index line of your compass, and then to look at the point on the compass dial *opposite* the index line. The number on the dial at this point is the back bearing (fig. 96). To follow this back bearing, set this number at the index line.

Another way of working with a back bearing is to set the original bearing at the index line, and position the direction of travel line to point at the back bearing by aligning the *south-seeking* end (the white or black end) of the magnetic needle with the pointed end of the declination arrow.

BEARINGS ON THE MAP

You can use your compass as a protractor, both to measure and to plot bearings on a map. Magnetic north and magnetic declination have nothing to do with these operations. Therefore, ignore the magnetic needle when measuring or plotting bearings on a map. (The only time you need to use the magnetic needle when working with the map is whenever you choose to orient the map to true north, explained later. But there is no need to orient the map to measure or plot bearings.)

To measure a bearing on a map: Place the compass on the map with the long edge of the base plate running between the two points of interest, as shown in figure 97. To measure the bearing from point A to point B, make sure the direction of travel line is pointing parallel to the direction from A to B (not the reverse). Then turn the rotating housing until its set of meridian lines is parallel to the north–south lines of the map. Be sure that the N on the compass dial is toward the top of the map and that the S is toward the bottom. (If you put the N toward the bottom of the map, with the S toward the top, your reading will be 180° off.) For the utmost in accuracy, slide the compass along the bearing line so that one of its meridian lines is exactly on top of one of the north–south lines on the map. Now read the number that is at the index line. This is the bearing from point A to point B.

Suppose you are at the summit of Panic Peak, and you want to know which of the many peaks around you is Deception Dome. Your map shows both peaks (fig. 97), so you can measure the bearing from point A, Panic Peak, to point B, Deception Dome. The result, as read at the index line, is 34°. (In this figure, we have purposely omitted the magnetic needle for the sake of clarity.) You can then hold the compass out in front of you and turn your entire body until you box the needle. The direction of travel line will then point toward Deception Dome and you can identify it.

To plot a bearing on the map: In this case you are starting with a known bearing. And where does that bearing come from? From a GO direction displayed on the GPS receiver's screen, or from an actual landscape compass reading. Let us take a hypothetical example: Your friend returns from a backpacking trip, remorseful for having left a camera

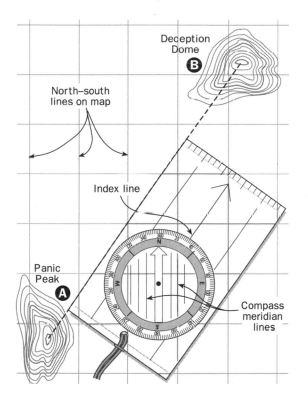

Figure 97.
Measuring a
bearing on a
map with the
compass as
a protractor
(magnetic
needle omitted
for clarity)

somewhere along the trail. While at a rest stop, your friend had taken a bearing on Mount Magnificent and found it to be 130°. That is all you need to know. You are heading into that same area next weekend, so get out the Mount Magnificent quadrangle, and here is what you do:

First set the bearing of 130° at the compass index line. Place the compass on the map, one long edge of the base plate touching the summit of Mount Magnificent (fig. 98). Rotate the entire compass (not just the housing) until the meridian lines in the compass housing are parallel with the map's north–south lines, and make sure that the edge of the base plate is still touching the summit. Again, make sure that the N on the compass dial is toward the top of the map. Draw a line along the edge of the base plate. Where this line crosses the trail is where your friend's camera is (or was).

When measuring or plotting bearings on a map, the map does not need to be in any particular position, such as lying down on the snow or dirt, on a stump, or in the mud. Instead, it can be vertical or in any other position. Its orientation doesn't matter, since in this case you are merely using the compass as a protractor.

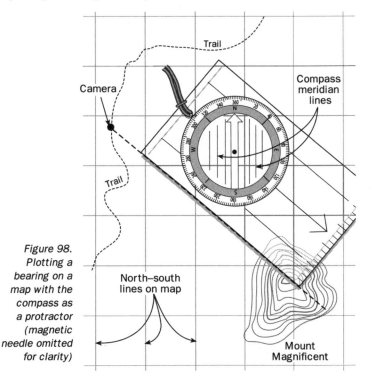

Figure 98. Plotting a bearing on a map with the compass as a protractor (magnetic needle omitted for clarity)

ORIENTING A MAP

During a trip it sometimes helps to hold the map so that north on the map is pointed in the actual direction of true north. This is known as *orienting the map*, a good way to obtain a better feel of the relationship between the map and the countryside.

One way to orient a map is by inspection: simply look at visible features in the terrain and compare them to the map. Then hold the map level and turn it until the map is lined up with the terrain.

This technique will not work if you cannot see any identifiable features around you. In this case, you can orient your map using your compass. Set 360° (north) at the index line of the compass and place your compass on the map. Put one long edge of the base plate along the left edge of the map, with the N of the compass dial pointing to the direction of north on the map. Then turn the map and compass together until the needle is boxed. The map is now oriented to the scene around you. (Map orientation can give you a general feel for the area but cannot replace the more precise methods of orientation that we covered in the preceding paragraphs.)

COMPASS ACCURACY AND ERRORS

If you ever doubt the accuracy of your compass—perhaps because it has developed a small bubble or has given you a questionable reading in the field—take it out to a street intersection where you know all the directions to test it. If the bearings you read are more than a few degrees away from the known correct bearings, consider replacing your compass.

You may have heard that nearby metal can influence a compass bearing. This is true. Ferrous objects such as iron and steel will deflect the magnetic needle and give false readings. Keep the compass away from belt buckles, ice axes, and other metal objects. Some wristwatches, particularly electronic ones, can also cause false readings if they are very close to the compass. If a compass reading does not make sense, check to see if nearby metal is sabotaging your bearing.

Keep your wits about you when pointing the direction of travel line and the declination arrow. If you point either of them backward—an easy thing to do—the reading will be 180° off. If the bearing is north, the compass will say it is south. Remember that the north-seeking end of the magnetic needle must be aligned with the pointed end of the declination arrow and that the direction of travel line must point from you to your objective.

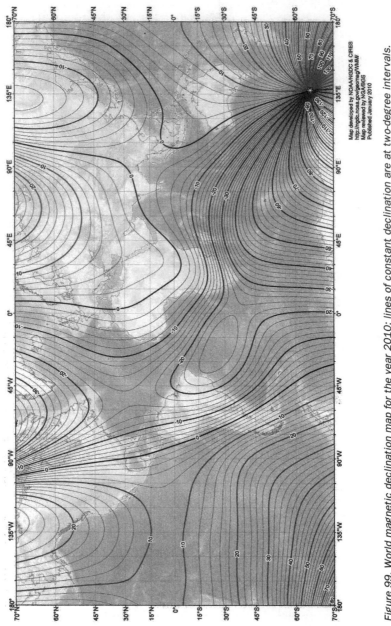

Figure 99. World magnetic declination map for the year 2010: lines of constant declination are at two-degree intervals. Positive numbers indicate east declination; negative numbers indicate west declination.

If in doubt, trust your compass. The compass, correctly used, is almost always right, while your contrary judgment may be clouded by fatigue, confusion, or hurry. If you get a nonsensical reading, check to see if perhaps you are making a 180-degree error. If not, and if no metal is nearby, verify the reading with other members of the party, using different compasses. If they get the same answer, trust your compass over hunches, blind guesses, and intuition.

WHERE TO GET DECLINATION INFORMATION

To find the declination for any point in the United States, you can call the USGS at 1-888-ASK-USGS. For Canada, call the Geological Survey of Canada at (613) 837-4241. Declination information is also available on the internet. The NOAA website, www.ngdc.noaa.gov/geomag -web/#declination, provides declination information for any place in the United States with only the postal ZIP code or the latitude/longitude coordinates of the location. The latter can be found by looking at any corner of a USGS topographic map for the area of interest.

Another useful website is the Canadian Geomagnetic Reference Field (CGRF), http://geomag.nrcan.gc.ca/calc/mdcal-eng.php. This will give you present declination for anywhere in North America when you enter a set of latitude and longitude coordinates. The CGRF can also give you declination for any year from 1960 to 2015; this time span is increased as time progresses.

In most parts of the world, you can buy topographic maps with declination information. If your travels bring you to a place where you cannot find the declination, and if you do not have access to a computer, you can find a fairly close estimate of the declination from the world declination map shown in figure 99.

CHANGES IN DECLINATION

Magnetic declination is caused by the motion of molten magnetic material in the earth's core. This motion is mostly random and unpredictable, so we cannot predict with certainty what the declination will be at any given place at some time far in the future. The best that geologists can do is to observe the present declination and the rate at which it is changing, and make predictions of what it will be only a very few years into the future.

In some areas, declination is changing by as much as 12 minutes, or 0.2 degree per year (one degree every five years). Keep this in mind whenever you are using a map that is more than a few years old. You should never rely on outdated information.

Bibliography

Burns, Bob, and Mike Burns. *Wilderness Navigation: Finding Your Way Using Map, Compass, Altimeter, and GPS.* 2nd ed. Seattle: Mountaineers Books, 2004.

DeLorme Earthmate PN-60 and PN-60w. *Instruction Manual and Quick Start Guide.*

Garmin eTrex 10, 20, and 30. *Instruction Manual and Quick Start Guide.*

Grubbs, Bruce. *Using a GPS: Digital Trip Planning, Recording, and Sharing. Backpacker Magazine* series. Guilford, Connecticut: FalconGuides, 2011.

Henderson, Dan. *Sea Kayaking: Basic Skills, Paddling Techniques, and Trip Planning.* Seattle: Mountaineers Books, 2012.

Letham, Lawrence, and Alex Letham. *GPS Made Easy.* Seattle: The Mountaineers Books, 2008.

Magellan eXplorist 510, 610, and 710. *Instruction Manual and Quick Start Guide.*

Matranga, Andrew. "Short Note Concerning Maximizing GPS Battery Life." *Backpacker Magazine* (September 2012), 50.

Index

About the Authors

A longtime member of The Mountaineers, **Bob Burns** has hiked, scrambled, climbed, and snowshoed extensively in Washington, Oregon, and California. He has been teaching classes in the use of map and compass since the late 1970s, not only for The Mountaineers courses but also for search-and-rescue groups and local schools. He is a coauthor of the "Navigation" chapter in *Mountaineering: The Freedom of the Hills,* 8th edition, after having been the chapter author for the fourth through seventh editions. He has also written articles on the use of GPS in wilderness travel (with son, Mike) and on Leave-No-Trace wilderness practices. He is a coauthor of *Wilderness Navigation,* a very successful book covering all relevant aspects of the use of maps, compasses, altimeters, and GPS receivers in the wilderness. It is used as a textbook for navigation courses taught by multiple branches of The Mountaineers. He has also taught GPS usage in The Mountaineers courses and seminars.

Mike Burns is a rock, ice, and expedition climber and filmmaker who has climbed in the Pacific Northwest, Colorado, Alaska, Canada, Mexico, Argentina, Nepal, Pakistan, and India, including a first ascent in the Himalaya. He has been an instructor and lecturer on the technical aspects of climbing, including navigation and GPS usage. He has written articles for *The Mountaineer* and *Climbing* magazines. He served on the revision committee for the seventh edition of *Mountaineering: The Freedom of the Hills,* after being a major contributor to the fifth and sixth editions of that book. He is also a coauthor of *Wilderness Navigation.*

recreation · lifestyle · conservation

MOUNTAINEERS BOOKS, including its two imprints, Skipstone and Braided River, is a leading publisher of quality outdoor recreation, sustainability, and conservation titles. As a 501(c)(3) nonprofit, we are committed to supporting the environmental and educational goals of our organization by providing expert information on human-powered adventure, sustainable practices at home and on the trail, and preservation of wilderness.

Our publications are made possible through the generosity of donors, and through sales of more than 500 titles on outdoor recreation, sustainable lifestyle, and conservation. To donate, purchase books, or learn more, visit us online:

MOUNTAINEERS BOOKS

Mountaineers Books
1001 SW Klickitat Way, Suite 201
Seattle, WA 98134
800-553-4453
mbooks@mountaineersbooks.org
www.mountaineersbooks.org

Leave No Trace strives to educate visitors about the nature of their recreational impacts and offers techniques to prevent and minimize such impacts. Leave No Trace is best understood as an educational and ethical program, not as a set of rules and regulations. For more information, visit www.lnt .org or call 800-332-4100.